Spoken Without a Word

Elly Sienkiewicz

Dedication/In Memoriam

Eileen Mary Clare-Patton (Pat) Hamilton Wigner

b. October 3, 1915 at Cross Park, Brixham, Devon, England
d. November 18, 2010 at Merwick, Princeton, NJ, United States

Dearest Mummy,

I did not have your talent. The Lord gave me health, time, support . . . to live out youthful dreams once held by you: The cherished "Our First Garden" pen and ink, the hasty hand-written poem on faith—'beauty's relics.' Such artist/author dreams you set unflinchingly aside for duty and for love. Daddy, children, grandchildren, great-grandchildren—all born to Liberty in this Land-of-milk-and-honey, all blossomed under your care.

To life's sweet end, you signed off evening calls—*and may you have a happy day, tomorrow.* Your grace, immortal, echoes in the hills & hollers of our lives—now a sweet remembrance, now a badge of steely courage, now your colleen laughter: all bringing our souls to smile.

From matriarch to Clan Hamilton icon—you are as one, now, with family Thanksgiving's-remembered elders: Your cultured *English* conjoins Daddy's *Vermont-farmer*-American, May Davina's *stalwart Scottish,* and indentured servant John Corbly's Irish lad *cum American hero*. What a lady, Mom! Amazing, strong, a lady forever; forever beloved.

—*Your El*

Spoken Without a Word
*A Lexicon of Selected Symbols
with 24 Patterns from Classic
Baltimore Album Quilts*

Elly Sienkiewicz

30th Anniversary Revised Edition—
A Baltimore Album Revival
Commemorative

Publication Manager: Teri A. Young
Copyeditor/Proofreader: Cornerstone
Creations, LLC
Cover Design: Susan H. Hartman
Book Design: Susan H. Hartman
Illustrator: Elly Sienkiewicz
Published by Turtle Hill Press®, LLC,
Washington, DC 20015, U.S.A.

Attention Copy Shops: Author and publisher give the owner of this book permission to photocopy pattern pages, 1@ pp. 32–36 and 58–107 for personal use only.

Attention Teachers: Author and publisher are pleased to have you use this book as a teaching text. See two quilts made entirely from patterns presented in this edition of *SWAW* in pictorial quilt gallery. Enjoy the many individual *SWAW* blocks set into larger pattern collections. Prefer to teach a whole small quilt? *SWAW* sports two unique, previously unpublished Wall Quilt patterns! Book's stunning photos model your class. Students, of course, must take patterns directly from book.

To order books:
www.createspace.com/3818091
Wholesale purchases available through Ingram or Baker & Taylor.

Library of Congress Cataloging-in-Publication Data
[Spoken without a word]

Spoken Without a Word
A Lexicon of Selected Symbols with 24 Patterns From Classic Baltimore Album Quilts
Elly Sienkiewicz
30th Anniversary Revised Edition—A Baltimore Album Revival Commemorative

ISBN-13: 978-0615717807 (Turtle Hill Press)
ISBN-10: 0615717802

[1. Applique – Patterns. 2. Album Quilts – Maryland – Baltimore. 3. Symbols. 4. History]

Book and cover design by Susan H. Hartman of Suett Communications

Cover: On left, Butterfly Medallion Center Pattern 16, designed by Eileen Mary Clare-Patton Hamilton-Wigner, 1983. On right, pattern transformed with appliqué and stitchery by Bette Florette Augustine: pattern reduced to 10″ × 10″ with finished block 12″ × 12″ square; silk fabrics, YLI silk thread (appliqué/embroidery/quilting), rayon threads, wire. Half-title page designed by Susan and Ed Hartman. Photograph by Ed Hartman.

𝓘n retrospect, one cannot be interested in an ancient tongue spoken, wordless, on cloth—without reconsidering the world around her, the images stitched, the human stories conveyed. Nor can she consider the history thus recorded—without curiosity about whence she came, who she has become. *Spoken Without a Word* is about needlework, old patterns, art, that having touched us, is being stitched anew today. In the broader sense, these designs, their history—all are fundamentally about you and me, our roots, our story—they are what has made us what we have become.

Table of Contents

PART III

Building Blocks in Baltimore's Album Monument   108

"Ah, how good it feels! The hand of an old friend."
—*Henry Wadsworth Longfellow*

THIRTY YEARS AGO, SEEDS from flower gardens of the 1800s were tenderly planted in the hearts and minds of contemporary quiltmakers by a visionary forever ahead of her time. In 1983, with the self-publishing of Elly Sienkiewicz's now famed red-covered book, *Spoken Without a Word*, we moderns began to see Baltimore's beloved Albums of the 1840s and '50s—as through a "window to the soul of the makers." The symbolism—both in carefully selected colors and in motif designs—conveyed their lives and times, making of these quilts "treasure troves of beauty and history." By their stitches, they shall be remembered. We'll now enjoy the depths of their stories for years to come. In our troubled whirlwind world, their clarion witness to courage, faith, hope, and love continues to comfort and uplift.

A symbolic tongue those Albums spoke, Elly suggested softly: That language only recently lost, she said, was *just beyond our memory*. Tucking a dictionary into her book, she shared these icons' ancient meanings. Her lectures followed: color-filled photos brought Victorian symbol-fluency to life. Each symbol stitched in cloth appeared, paired with its sister emblem, painstakingly graveyard-carved, in stone. In so many ways, Elly opened our eyes and hearts to these quilts. Those seeds she had planted in *Spoken Without a Word* began to take root, grow, and bloom. Thirty years later, this generation's love of those Baltimore Albums that had so intrigued Elly in this first 1983 book has blossomed in a multitude of blocks and quilts, each with its own story to tell.

The excitement over this 30th anniversary edition of *Spoken Without a Word* is as joyfully anticipated as the birth of a grandchild. The inspiration *Spoken Without a Word* has offered needleartists for 30 years now will long inspire stitchers, encouraging them to carry the cherished historic traditions that are "The Baltimores" into their lives . . . and into the future.

In the 1980s, my sister introduced me to the beauty of the Baltimores. She had lovingly stitched intricate blocks, some of which were personally designed to tell her own story. Although immensely admiring of her embellished handwork and intrigued by the unique red-covered book inspiring her, I never thought I, myself, could accomplish such beautiful works of art. Years passed. My interest in machine work transferred to a passion for handwork appliqué and embroidery. The memories of my sister's quilt blocks surfaced and inspired me. And so my journey began.

I met Elly in 2003 at the North Carolina Quilters Symposium, under the Magnolias. A long-lasting, treasured friendship began, and her loving mentoring and encouragement have inspired me these past ten years as a needleartist, designer, teacher, and author. She has gifted me with the confidence to believe in my ability to create and stitch an album uniquely my own.

Elly's encouragement and confidence are gifts she offers freely to all she meets, in person . . . and through the pages of her books. *Spoken Without a Word* is a legacy-gift from Elly to you and me and to future generations. As you walk hand in hand with our beloved friend, Elly, through the pages of *Spoken Without a Word*, whether as a new friend or old, may you continue to be blessed, encouraged, motivated, and inspired for many years to come.

—*Jan Vaine*
June 10, 2012
Jacksonville, Florida

EDITOR'S NOTE: Jan Vaine was The Guest Artist for Ancillary Projects in Elly's *Baltimore Elegance—A New Approach to Classic Album Quilts* (2006). She has since authored best-selling *The Art of Elegant Hand Embroidery, Embellishment and Appliqué* (2011), *Appliqué & Embroidery Fundamentals* (2012), *Ribboned Bouquet* (2012), and *Needle Grace—Cloth, Ribbon and Thread* (2013). Enjoy Jan's latest publications, *Embroidery & Patchwork Revisited* (2014) and *Hand Embroidery Stitches at a Glance* (2014). Visit www.grahamcrackercollection.com for more information about her books, patterns, teaching schedule and biannual *Tea & Stitches Retreat* in Jacksonville, Florida.

Cover to the Memorial Service for Donald Ross Hamilton, 6 January 1972.
Pen and Ink drawing by Eileen Hamilton, March 1944. Donald and Eileen
are author's parents.

> *"The pen and ink drawing symbolizes the turn of the season;*
> *the center representing spring,*
> *the outer circle fall.*
> *From our first garden,*
> *Floral Park, Long Island."*
>
> —Eileen Hamilton

RITA MACIONA

Preface

Honoring Baltimore's Album Movement

BEYOND BALTIMORE—BECAUSE BEAUTY MATTERS . . . When a modern, 30 years ago, entered the vintage realm of Baltimore's Album Quilts, she crossed ring after ring of iconic quilt genres, each more splendid and interesting than that which she had met before. She was used to greatness of scale, having resonated to patiently pieced Log Cabins, constellations of Lone Stars, the nostalgia of Grandmother's Flower Gardens, the sheer mass of humble nine-patches. She had sensed devout dreams clothed in white-on-white, then · quilted, stuffed, and brought to life. She had felt awe at block names' witness to panoramic history (Rake, Kansas Troubles, Delectable Mountains) by which courageous quilt-makers, forgers of our nation, had stitched their souls to hers. And yet, after passing through America's most monumental needle-work, she was impressed above all by appliqué, an art of infinite expanse, the end of which she could not see, no matter in which direction she looked.

This day, 150 years and more later, Baltimore's Antebellum Albums float at the peak of quiltmakers' imaginations. Unlike Baltimore—the city that defined and gave these quilts her name—*The who? The why? The how?* of these magical quilts had vanished. Much of the "how" of making these quilts has been recovered, but their making-context, until recently, has remained obscured. Increasingly, those old master-pieces have new-born daughters, some rivaling their mothers' glory. Like sisters, they differ: changed if Japanese-pallette created; changed again if in Australia born. Same genre, Revivalist Baltimore style, but different. All beauty, Aristotle noted, is a gift from God. These Beauties made not with overweening ambition, but with the greatest humility, and on a quiet, womanly scale, in caring homes, as comforting cradles of simplest gifts, best gifts; these Beauties have inspired anew.

Questions (fascination's witness) linger. We moderns have devised ways to echo slow roller-printing's shaded effects (call them as you will: *ombrés*, rainbows, or *fondues*); we've mastered printers' die-stamped banderoles, cartouches, too—by tracing or ironed-on transfers. We can even sign in Copperplate, old time's "tall, un-embellished" hand. *Who? Why? Those questions still enthrall.* In the 1990s (within Revivalists' lifetimes), the World Wide Web was born. Quilters grew quickly to be the largest early 'special-interest-users'.[1] The original-source quilt information has since burgeoned. No researcher could have imagined today's wealth of resources twenty years ago.[2]

---

1 Conversation with a Reuters Correspondent at a conference on Journalists and the Web, at Washington, DC's National Press Club. Responding to my having identified myself as a quilt book author, the journalist exclaimed, "Did you know quilters are the fastest-growing special-interest group on the Web?" For this conference topic to have been timely, it would have been post-1995, given the Web's history . . . but not by much. That the world's quilters so quickly formed community on the World Wide Web must say something significant about the intelligence and skills of those quilters. 19th Century America called this principled striving "self-improvement" and in the self-education era of Lincoln and Henry Clay—just *before* public schooling—it put the U.S. at the pinnacle of Western countries' literacy rates.

2 Interesting that the contemporary quiltworld's intense web-connection had such early roots!

Baltimore's Album Revival was not expected to be what it has become. We thought it would produce much in artistry recognized, techniques revealed, history shared, women's lives affirmed; but not the hundreds of quilts, thousands of blocks, dimensional flowers piling a quarter of a mile high, and thread stitched so doggedly that it could wrap our Planet Earth 'round and 'round again. We expected a revival of unfathomable numbers, but numbers of leaves and stems and bows and berries, rather than of masterpiece quilts, boundless squares, Baltimore block-carrying cases, masters' classes, Album stitching "Bees"—friendship groups, appliqué guilds, burning enthusiasms, and stitchers across the world joined through and through by shared joy and silent understandings.

Nonetheless, this great inventory of quilts, blocks, books, teachers, class-takers, technique, lives recorded, friendships cemented, and quiltmakers-bound-internationally into community is what we now have. A Revival founded on a vision of beauty, both group and individually crafted, has become a subculture of decades-long duration. A Revival founded in humble aspirations has become an enduring movement of substantial influence.

When the Baltimore Album Revival was 1980s young, our modern stitcher studied the classic quilts, searching out their symbols' meanings, helped perhaps by *Spoken Without a Word's* Lexicon of Symbols. She sought to learn the quilts' 'technology' so that she herself might follow their artists' needlework journey. Today we have studied that Album style deeply and well. We have exploited its techniques so effectively that the best contemporary quilts compare in accomplishment with the classic models that we yet approach in awe.[3] But all that remains uniquely "Baltimore" in those old quilts still matters: We have not forgotten their vivacious asymmetry, their warmth of character, their optimism, their joyous patriotism, their steady faithfulness, and their idealistic intent. Though we stitch in a style now "beyond Baltimore," we have accumulated rich stores from the Old Ones' beauty and decency. Our moral thirst, a thirst ever-slaked by the Albums' nobility, maintains the Baltimore Album Revival. In this vast Universe that is our home, we hunger to know that who we are and what we do matters. Baltimore's Albums are Beauty's wellspring of warmth, which reassure us that this is so.

Decades have passed. And yet "The Baltimores" continue to comfort souls. *Spoken Without a Word 1983* had become hard to find and expensive. A Celebratory Anniversary Revision with quilts, color, and reflective articles seemed a good idea. It should honor both the 'mother' Albums and their history-making 'daughters.' And of course that 'big red book' of old could nestle within the new. Your patience so appreciated, gentle reader[4], the original *SWAW's* pioneer-trail has been blazed, herein. Some

RITA MACIONA

---

3 Research shows most of the finest Baltimore Album Quilts to have been group made. The majority of Revivalist Albums entered in international competitions, though, are made by a single individual or the top designed and sewn by her, and the quilting professionally done. For an individual, rather than a group, to make such an Album is a stunning accomplishment by any measure! Even today, though, as one who has led multiple group Revivalist Albums, division of labor, each putting her all into her block, her sashing, or her border section, produces a collection of small gems in a masterful whole.

4 "gentle reader" [sic] is how Dr. William Rush Dunton addresses the reader in his 1946 self-published *Old Quilts*. I use it thus, within, as a small homage to Dr. Dunton, founder of Occupational Therapy and author of the first book dedicated to study of what has since been called "Baltimore Brides Quilts" and more recently, "Baltimore Album Quilts." His mother a devoted needlewoman (with work shown at the Philadelphia Centennial Exhibition), Dunton was consumed with the antebellum Baltimore-style Albums of Maryland. His manner is informal, chatty even, and companionable, as though he understands that his reader must similarly be interested in his encyclopedic detail. In homage to that warm, Album-fascinated man, the *gentle reader* is addressed within.

may find its cream-color pages familiar—though darkened, now, with age.

As for those antebellum Beauties...Did they matter in their day? Indeed. For they intended to be heard. They spoke without words and Americans of that day understood what they said. Less so, today. It is as though we have forgotten half the alphabet, and are limited to using only the words that we can construct from the remaining letters. So we must steep ourselves in that era's history and culture—to understand those quilts' archaic expressions.

Spirited, talented, driven, and entrepreneurial, the Ladies of Baltimore's quilt enterprises commanded press-worthy recognition. Circa 1845–52, they elevated Maryland's simpler Albums with sophisticated blocks, innovative sets and borders, even whole professionally High-Style Album Quilts. Tied to the Revolutionary generation; thrilled by the achievements of 'Progress,' yet fearful for national unity, they said important things, produced great art, (and probably earned a pretty, commercial penny in the process.) They employed tutored Art Principles, developed ingeniously realistic appliqué techniques—so creatively apparent, so clearly comprehended just by observing—then and now—that this life-changing style caught on. And the historic cause? Their voice was heard gentle reader, but there is more to their story, and it is my fondest hope to continue helping to tell it.[5]

BETTE AUGUSTINE

5 This Preface, written here to celebrate the Baltimore Album Revival's fourth decade begun, draws upon an essay that appeared in *The Best of Baltimore Beauties: 95 Patterns for Album Blocks and Borders*; Lafayette: C&T Publishing, Inc., 2000. It echoes themes of the author's opening Address given at the Awards Ceremony of the "Baltimore Album Legacy Exhibition," the Mancuso Brother's Conference in Santa Clara, California 1998. (Exhibition catalogue published as *Baltimore Album Legacy*.)

Introduction

"Through Tufts of Broidered Flowers," 2005–2009, by Susan Kurth and author; Stan and Elly Sienkiewicz at Sitges International Patchwork Festival, 2012.

VIEWING ANTIQUE QUILTS ON exhibition, I—all unexpecting—found soulmates. Early 1840s-50s, those *Old Ones* were boldly bright, almost flashy. Beauties they were; fascinating, but not my type. A tear brimmed in my eye. It puzzled me, for I did not know then that they were slipping into my soul. That was 1982 and now, 33 years later, I still love the antebellum Baltimore quilt style and its 'Beyond Baltimore' descendants. In 1982, though, practicality ruled my life: I mothered three children and managed two businesses. Bone tired, I struggled to be free of the businesses. Philosophical by nature, I had not asked a profound question for five years—not since right after my youngest had been born. Entrepreneurship and motherhood were in eclipse. I struggled to regain balance—and contentment. Who would have thought Albums would lead my way?

In retrospect, one cannot be interested in an ancient tongue spoken, wordless, on cloth—without reconsidering the world around her, the images stitched, the human stories conveyed. Nor can she consider the history thus recorded—without curiosity about whence she came, who she has become. *Spoken Without a Word* is about needlework, old patterns, art, that having touched us, is being stitched anew today. In the broader sense, these designs, their history—all are fundamentally about you and me, our roots, our story—they are what has made us what we have become.

My husband, Stan, and I are on a British Airways 777, returning from a sojourn in Sitges, Spain. My teaching invitation included a request for ten of my group-made Revivalist Baltimore Album Quilts for a solo exhibition at the Mediterranean's *Festival de International Patchwork*. Happily, Stan had been invited to accompany me—and the quilt cases. We are in delightful seats: right side, last row. Plane not half-full, we feel pampered. Extra dessert? "An ancient English recipe, a lemon posset"; a thimbleful of cognac; then strong tea, milky and sugared. Pavarotti's magnificent rendition of "La Boheme" streams through earphones. The water in my glass jostles, mimics the plane's shimmy-forward.

Stan calls me to his window. Below lies the Labrador Sea afloat with ice. We edge over dark mountainous land, frozen rivers, and see icy road-drawn geometric grids. He reminds me that before man could fly trans-Atlantic non-stop, planes stopped to refuel below at Gander Air Field. My soul twinkles a smile, recalling. So long have I loved this man, his thirst for the human story, his fascination with the natural world. That earliest woods-walk . . . courting. He'd spied, plucked, then offered a sprig of wintergreen, saying taste it, do you know

JOAN DORSAY

what this is? Learned it in Boy Scouts. I was older, a schoolteacher, he a college senior. It was refreshing, charming even.

A European sea-side quilt show with Revivalist Baltimores, inter-continental travel, viewing our earthly home from the air, anticipating the writing, thirty-odd years later, of a revised edition of my first book, one on a 19th century art form. Right now, though, I'm intrigued by my *en route* reading of Charles Murray's latest, *Coming Apart.* My fingers itch to record thoughts thus provoked. I recall that an earlier Murray book, *Human Accomplishment,*[1] hypothesized that it is a search for the Good, the True, and the Beautiful that makes artworks classic. 'Classic,' of course, denotes "setting a standard for all time." That proposition explained to me why so many of us derive transporting joy from creating, inspired by the now-classic style of antebellum Baltimore Album Quilts.

I had never written a book, but in 1983, *Spoken Without a Word* came easily, quickly, and with enthusiasm. Enthralled by these old quilts recently seen at exhibition[2] and coming to realize that they were speaking to us without words, I included a Lexicon of Symbols. My next three decades sang a Baltimorean Song as I learned this art's techniques. We became many inspiring

colleagues around the world—replicating and innovating "Revivalist Baltimore-Style Albums"—'til this research, writing, and quilt-making has become an enduring movement. Is it conceivable those quilts may come to be recognized as a Revivalist art movement, or as a "Turn of the Century *'school of art'*"?

As I worked, I followed an enticing trail, researching historical questions in old books, and later, on the so-accessible World Wide Web. To feed my soul, I studied the faith of those first Album ladies, and for my joy, I taught in a paradise of grown-ups, mostly women, all of us thrilled to be walking this fascinating path. Murray, in *Human Accomplishment,* suggests why such artwork, such study is so fulfilling, why it makes *us* all so happy—proposing that for art to have meaning for the future it must contain something of the transcendent. His supposition rings true. The quiet optimism and underlying faith of Murray's hypothesis has fed my soul in the same way that stitching and studying the Old Ones has. For those Antebellum Baltimore Albums shine with gratitude. Gratitude for shelter, food, friends, and family: for all God's good gifts—each day, here in Liberty's Land.

Spoken Without a Word 2014 (SWAW 2014), **too,** is gratitude's offering for the Albums, both the old and the new. It brings *Spoken*

1 Charles Murray, *Human Accomplishment: The Pursuit of Excellence in the Arts and Sciences, 800 B.C. to 1950,* (AEI Press, 2004.) *Coming Apart*: The State of White America, 1960–2010 is this political scientist's 2012 book, referred to in passing.

2 *Baltimore Album Quilts*, by Dena Katzenberg is that exhibition's elegant catalogue. It gives show dates and itinerary:
   • The Museum of Fine Art, Houston 11.18.1980 – 1.11.1981
   • The Metropolitan Museum of Art, NY 6.30 – 8.30.1981
   • The Baltimore Museum of Art 12.13.1981 – 2.7.1982

JOAN DORSAY

JOAN DORSAY

Without a Word 1983 back into print and much augmented.[3] Written for quiltmakers and designed as a pattern book introduction to Baltimore's Albums, that volume combined historical inquiry with quilt-making technique. Its 1983 publication date caught the excitement aroused by the just closed 1982 Baltimore Museum of Art traveling exhibition, "Baltimore Album Quilts." True to *SWAW1983*, this present edition does not 'correct' theories about the pre-Civil War *Baltimores*, not even theories since found to have been insufficiently substantiated. For history's sake, such initial 'misunderstandings' appear just as they did in the original text and Pattern Notes.[4] The informative Lexicon remains original text. Its symbols' brief meanings had been culled from enduring Western Civilization sources dating back to Biblical times. Some symbol definitions were culled from post-Album era genre books on the Victorian 'Secret Language of the Flowers.'

～∽ ～∽ ～∽

The Commemorative Arts

"To cherish the recollection of those who have lived an ornament and benefit to the world, or a delight to their immediate connexions [sic], is not only a duty we owe to their memory, but an advantage to ourselves . . . to perpetuate these feelings of admiration and affection, by some lasting memento of their worth . . ."
—John Mills, Architect, 1820

The early 19th Century surged with social and economic change, change that re-awakened the Commemorative Arts. Passionate interest in these arts was manifested in the "Rural Cemetery Movement" —a new approach to cemeteries; a patriotic wave of public monument-building; and, I would suggest, manifested as well in Baltimore's Album Quilts. All these were abetted by an increasingly wealthy middle class with more leisure time, more discretionary income. Our Revivalist quilts, too, so many overtly commemorative, are art requiring time and money.

Though the Albums record wars and deep personal loss, though their makers lived in times of sweeping transformation and still widespread hardship, their tone is eager with faith-filled excitement at the Industrial Revolution that was dramatically changing lives for the better. We seldom stop to think that it produced the greatest rise in living standards since the secret of agriculture was discovered. Grateful, Album-makers applauded the good in it, and while their lives remained harder than

---

3 *Spoken Without a Word II, Baltimore's Antebellum Albums, History and Hypotheses,* Elly Sienkiewicz, forthcoming. For availability, watch www.AppliqueWithElly.com and Amazon.com.

4 One such misconception, however, in "the single album artist attributions," begins to be reassessed in the research paper: "Dr. Dunton, Mary Evans, and the Baltimore Album Quilt Attributions." [p 109]

EDIE ZAKEM

ours (penicillin not yet discovered), they sing a joyful song. There is *no whining*—in their quilts.

❧ ❧ ❧

Were Antebellum Baltimores an Art School, an Art Movement?

History must remain the judge. Usually named in retrospect, Art 'Schools' and Art 'Movements' have in common "shared ideas, philosophy, and goals." These artist group 'intentions' or messages are their *intangibles*. Their tangibles are "using the same unique techniques and sometimes, but not always, sharing the same location." These criteria define an Art School or Movement. Don't decades of studying the unique *How?* of these classic Albums, leave us curious about their *Why?* Sensing that they spoke through Fine Art's ancient symbolic coin originally led to this book's Lexicon. Basic, that worked well as a dictionary for the early 1840's Baltimore Albums. Their iconography was as simple as one appliquéd motif, and often one likely meaning. Mid Album Era, though, the appliqué shapes became dramatically more layered both with appliques and with meanings. The symbols were more complex and, subsequent research shows, helped define a subject as specific as a famous person. Once understood—we must assume—stitched themes of great public interest would have quickly become recognizable to such a quilt's contemporaries.

Complex blocks in intelligibly organized sets were then presented with framing borders. "High-style," Katzenberg dubbed the finest of these Albums. In citing rough dates, "1846–1852," she, knowingly or not, linked Baltimore's peak Album production to historic events—events that were searing that city's soul. Does this mean that if we can 'crack the symbol code,' we can hope to 'read' the increasingly activist Ladies of Baltimore's increasingly complex blocks? Can we know—as fellow-citizens clearly did—of what and whom their art in silence speaks? Fascinating questions—requiring that both our lexicon and our story continue at a later time. For us now, "Does our modern movement share a common goal with the Old Ones, and if it does, what might it be?" Please consider that question as you enjoy this book's stitched excellence, its Revival Era essays, its thoughtful artist-penned commentary.

Increasing evidence points to High-Style Baltimores as reflecting all the criteria for being an *Art School* or *Movement* with common methods, messages, and goals. Can we also name the most artistically outstanding of our Revivalist Baltimore Albums the products of the "Turn of the Century (20th-21st) High-Style Baltimore Album Movement?" Certainly, it shares same timeframe, skills, techniques, subject matter, and aspirations toward beauty, and even transcendence. But *not* location. *Revivalist* 'geography' is the *industrialized* world, marked by translated manuals and patterns in abundance, traveling teachers, conferences, brick & mortar stores as well

as virtual quilt shops—all offering skilled professional Album teaching. In guilds and stitching groups, Album makers learn from each other in joyous contagion around the world. The production of these contemporary quilts began in the early 1980's and continues today. This body of work's earliest disseminators were, as their Baltimorean sisters, Americans—but Revivalism has quickly spread throughout the industrialized world and signs are that its growing edge is outside the U.S.[5]

The Contemporary Revivalist Baltimore Movement is many things to many people. The 'human accomplishment' reflected in the Baltimore Albums, which bloomed then and blooms again today, is a product not so much of teaching women "the knowledges, sciences and trades," nor even the arts, but of their own determination to pursue the Good, the True, and the Beautiful. This sentiment from the 19th century we share today.

As for me, I've been ever grateful to walk in your company these happy decades. Without you this contemporary Baltimore Revival movement could not be so dear to me. Mindful of these gifts, I've come to think of this 30th Anniversary Edition as though it were a metaphorical 'monument' to Baltimore Albums, all. Let this monument's foundation be *SWAW*'s Original Edition, its artists' building blocks its art works, its mortar its essays through these constructive decades. To use John Mills's felicitous phrasing, we are recording the worth in Antebellum Baltimores, paying a tribute here to this Revivalist Movement's great outpouring of beauty.

This edition, as all my books, could not have come to be without your contributions. It honors *you, the generous needleartists,* even as it does our antebellum sisters. For you have learned old Baltimore's Album attributes and stitched them into glorious renaissance and more. So many many of you, gentle reader, have shared your beautiful Albums on exhibition, in class, in magazines. Would that those could be pictured in one place! So many have shared your written expression, stitched blocks, quilts—all labors of love, gratefully enjoyed.

We've walked together, gentle reader, from my days as a young mother writing in the deep of night, to the children in my life being my children's children, and my bedtime now so early. Little time is allotted to us in this life, but what joy you and this communion of quilts have given me. How fast it has flown! But what a privilege it has been.

EDIE ZAKEM

---

5 As an example, I first started teaching as a stay at home mother, from my Washington, DC bedroom. I began to travel to teach after *SWAW*'s 1983 publication. I traveled infrequently at first, but as my children grew, I came to teach as often as once a month, predominantly in the US, and often in Canada. Ultimately, I traveled three times to the Netherlands and Belgium, twice to New Zealand, as well as once each to Japan and South Africa.

Part I

Gallery of Quilts

PHOTO: ROLAND DORSAY

"3 of 1" by Joan Dorsay (64.5" × 64.5")

"A Baltimore Reflection" by Rosalynn McKown (82″ × 82″)

" *Really good works of art reveal something new each time we enjoy them. The Baltimore Album Quilts are unique in the depth of their beauty, complexity, and symbolism. As we learn more about them, our appreciation only intensifies.*"

—Rosalynn McKown

PHOTO: GREGORY CASE PHOTOGRAPHY

"New York Baltimore" by Dawn Licker

"The care, love, detail work, and beauty of these quilts seem in every stitch to show a piece of the woman's soul who made them."

—Ardeth "Ardie" Sveadas,
TESAA Challenge winner, 2012

"There has always been a mystery surrounding the Baltimore Album Quilts. The more mature quilters appreciate the length of time it takes to make one of these quilts."

—Delia P. Kane

Beth Jensen

"The Fabric of Our Lives" by Leslie Stevenson (107" × 106")

"A Touch of Raspberry" by Fiona Lindsay

"BAQs were made and meant as a celebration of life and friends. You can still sense the joy."
—Rita Verroca

PHOTO: GUY HOLLING

"*The BAQ has a nostalgic mystique about it. The quest for the unknown keeps it going. Each time I stitch I wonder: Who did this before me? What was it that they were thinking as they stitched? Who were these ladies? What was their life's story? Oh, so many questions to ponder.*"
—Mary Ann (Carvelho) Bloom

"Baltimore Recollection" by Rita Maciona (87" × 87")

"What draws me to a pattern are the focus features that tug at my heart: flowers and animals. I love to create blocks and to add as many details as I can to draw people in. I want to hear them say, 'Wow! How did she do that?' Baltimore Album blocks are a perfect canvas for this."
—Mary K. Tozer

"Memories of Wales" by Ann Nash (94″ × 94″)

"Music My Rampart" by Mildred Tahara (91″ × 91″)

"Finding moments in one's busy life to stitch a block means setting aside personal time both physically and mentally—providing introspection directed toward both the work and outward to the stitcher's life journey. Through appliqué, our voices are clear and filled with joy!"

—Bette F. Augustine

"The Zehr-Esch Baltimore Quilt" by Janet Zehr Esch

"How can I describe the emotional experience of first seeing something that has its birth in the home of a woman who, with few tools and little other than natural light, painstakingly created quilts of such beauty. The answer is simple: we are not only preserving their work, but the BAQs connect us to them, and to our past. We want to become one with them. Our breath becomes slowed when we work, faster when we look at their stitching, and fastest when we actually touch the quilt and the fabric itself."

—Janet Zehr Esch, *President (2013–14) of The Baltimore Appliqué Society, international by web from the Baltimore Maryland region.*

"To have a connection (because of Elly) to the women who created these designs so many years ago and the impact it has had on so many of us is truly a blessing."
—Karen Pessia

PHOTO: JEFFREY LOMICKA

"My Baltimore Journey" by Karen Pessia

"Americana Baltimore Quilt" by Wendy Grande (60" × 60")

Baltimore Album Quilts are pieces of art that bring joy and happiness to all who see them and to all who attempt to imitate them. By studying them, we have a view of our nation's past social, economic, and political systems."

—Delia P. Kane

"Never Again . . . Again" by
Joan Dorsay (62.5″ × 62.5″)

"My Baltimore"
by Janet Gunn Sewell (76″ × 93″)

PHOTO: KIMBERLY RASHED; ASSISTANT, DAVID RASHED

"Love's Journey" by Edie Zakem (69″ × 69″)

"I love the joy of creating each little jewel."
—Gena Holland

"To create in the Baltimore Album style makes us a part of something larger. We feel an affinity with the makers of the original Baltimores as well as a sisterhood with those contemporaries who, too, are creating 'revivalist' quilts."

—Rosalynn McKown

"Best of Friends—A Reverse Appliqué Sampler" by Linda Bear (80″ × 80″)

"I believe the beauty, originality, and history of the ladies who started the Baltimore Album Quilts are still influencing women today—almost as if they have stretched their arms to our generation to continue this unique journey, which is quilting."

—Karen Moraal

"Out of Many One—*E Pluribus Unum***" by Mildred Tahara** (91″ × 91″)

"Aloha Ula—Love Red" by Kansas Capital Quilt Guild (95″ × 95″)

"In today's busy world with 'fast everything' around us, we women know the precious time spent on these quilts and their journeys are worth more than diamonds and gold."
—Katherine Scott Hudgins Dunigan

Sandra Reynolds
copyright applied for

PHOTO: SANDRA REYNOLDS

"My Tree of Life" designed by Sandra Reynolds
(75″ × 75″ with patterned 36-inch square center medallion)

Dream Garden

Designed by Dawn Licker; finished quilt 40-inches square, with 24-inch center medallion, inner border has two rows of 2-inch colored squares and outer borders 4-inches wide with appliquéd vines and leaves.

Corner

Repeat *Border*

© Rita Verroca 2012

Rita Verroca's Friendship Quilt Border Pattern; finished quilt
92-inches square, with 18-inch blocks and 10-inch wide border.

Spoken Without a Word

"Rita Verroca Friendship Quilt" by Rita's Club led by Rita Verroca (92″ × 92″ with 18-inch blocks and 10-inch wide border). All block patterns within *SWAW2014*. Border pattern, page 35.

PHOTO: STEVIE VERROCA

*Spoken
Without a Word*

by Elly Sienkiewicz

Acknowledgements

ORIGINAL 1983 EDITION

TWO GROUPS OF PEOPLE made this book possible. One is the exceptional staff at Cabin Fever Calicoes who virtually ran that business during the writing of this book. The other is my husband, Stan, and children, Donald, Alex, and Katya, who gave help, support, encouragement, and took on much of the business of housekeeping, even on vacation. To all of them, a very special Thank You. Two very good friends were invaluable as well. They are: Valerie Howard who took my daughter while the boys were at camp, leaving me free to work, and Nancy Wischnowski, who gave careful advice on this text and loaned me her precious copy of Dunton's Book.

I also wish to acknowledge my gratitude to the artists who both inspired and contributed to this work. They are my mother and the women who designed and executed the classic Baltimore Album Quilts. Without them this book would never have come to be.

My mother, Eileen Mary Clare-Patton Hamilton-Wigner, entwined my childhood and that of my brother and sister with lovely things. The loveliest of all was her radiant smile, but beyond that were daily touches of beauty which gave all three of us that love for artistry which has so enriched our lives.

"Mummy" expresses her deepest feelings best by making beautiful things and "doing for" those who are privileged to have her touch their lives. She is unexcelled in both her Art and her caring. The symbolic pen and ink drawing which is the Frontispiece of this book shows the devotion to detail in her artistic labors; and my father was, he said, "a happy man, a lucky man" under her loving care, despite a thirty year bout with multiple sclerosis. (Of her smile he said, "As a young man I was shy; but I blossomed under your mother's smile as a flower opens to the sun.")

My mother is still "doing for" others. Last Spring, after only hours notice she stayed to care for my young family while I traveled for several days to lecture. Desperately behind, I asked her to organize my slides for the talk which was on Baltimore Album Quilts. Though not a quiltmaker herself, those nine-teenth century appliqués so caught her imagination that several weeks later she mailed me the exceptional block, "Butterfly Medallion," whose pattern is number 16. It is a design of such well-executed originality that it rivals the most talented of the classic designers upon whose legacy it builds. And as ever, her caring and her artistry went hand in hand: exacting, industrious, exceptionally fine expressions of a somewhat reserved but very full heart. How good to be able still to say, Thank You, Mummy.

Clearly, the beauty of the Baltimore Album Quilts captured my heart and impelled the production of this book. But their "heart" captured me as well. For the depth of feeling which goes into creating such laborious and masterful works of art must reflect the same dedication I have seen in my mother; I recognize it expressed in the best works of these almost anonymous women artists. Reproducing the patterns presented in this book was a painstaking enterprise. What took hours and hours to capture in pen and ink, printed screens and glue, must surely have taken days and days to create in needle and thread. Beyond this impressive patience, the design skill and creativity apparent in superior Baltimore Album Quilt Blocks is truly breathtaking.

The patterns replicated here are faithful hand-drawn representations of actual blocks from classic 1843–1852 Baltimore Album Quilt blocks. They are intended for contemporary use and reflect my admiration for the peerless appliqué displayed in these quilts.

I have often wondered how the women who designed these blocks would feel knowing they had become so popular as to be reproduced in books such as this, well over a century later. Actually, there is evidence that some of the patterns originating in the decades of the 1840s and 1850s, or the blocks and finished quilts, were produced on commission or for outright sale. It is none-the-less my hope that what might have been considered an intrusion upon an artist's market by a contemporary quilt designer, will emerge softened by time as the inevitable culmination of genius: history's accolade.

It is a loss, though, to have no names to attach with confidence to this windfall heritage now so popular. The modesty of these gifted women seems, from our perspective, more poignant than charming. But perhaps it is best that we try to meet them where they stood, to try to understand the passions which impelled them and the fulfillments they found, from their art alone. To say simply, and with feeling, Thank You, whoever you are, for this gift of beauty.

KAREN PESSIA

To Stan
Whose Russian Soul makes the Victorians Real

Author's Preface

ORIGINAL 1983 EDITION

MANY A QUILTMAKER BEGINS by making a pillow or two, not believing she will ever make a quilt. That is how this book began.

My first introduction to the Baltimore Album Quilts was the full page color photograph of an Album Quilt block as the frontispiece of Bishop and Safanda's *America's Quilts and Coverlets* published in 1972. From then on these quilts intrigued me.

The block depicted an epergne of fruit. One particular question haunted me for years. The fruit and its container were shaded with three-dimensional effect. But how was it done? Was it painted? Was it velveteen? (The objects looked so rich and contoured.) Clearly pen and ink were used for many details, but there was no convincing clue to the enigma, and no books with further information that I knew of.

Oddly, perhaps, it was this question most of all which prompted me to accept the invitation of a dear friend and neighborhood quilt expert, Sue Hannan, to visit the exhibit of 24 Baltimore Album Quilts at the Baltimore Museum of Art in 1982.

I was unprepared for the impact of that show of quilts. The compelling beauty of the Baltimore Album Quilt was undeniable—and more. For the Baltimore Album Quilt genre is truly the "Fascinating Lady" of our American Quilt Heritage. There was also the answer to my question: Preprinted shaded cotton fabrics were used extensively in these quilts. But for

every question answered, more were raised. The quilts are treasure troves, not only of beauty, but of social and cultural history. They are a window to the soul of the women who made them.

Spoken Without a Word began as a pattern series: I wanted to convey the depth of detail in those unrivaled appliqué blocks and provide patterns as good as the originals. The close scrutiny required led almost inevitably to a study of the symbolism in the motifs which characterize these quilts. And like the quiltmaker who realizes that having made so many pillows she could have made a quilt, it became clear that the material I had gathered had grown into a book.

As this goes to press, yet more beautiful and symbolically significant Album Quilt blocks tempt me. It is in the nature of the Baltimore Album Quilt genre, in fact, it is one of its most appealing attributes, that while the wealth of its varied themes lures one's curiosity, its distance in time veils the quest with mystery. The reader is invited to join *Spoken Without a Word* in pursuing an acquaintance with that Fascinating Lady of bygone Baltimore. You will no doubt find her a devout creature of highest moral character, warm sympathies, and great beauty. You may never be sure you really know her, but you will never forget her.

—*Elly Sienkiewicz*
Washington, D.C. October, 1983

Introduction

SPOKEN WITHOUT A WORD is a wee Lexicon of selected symbols, and their meanings, from the Baltimore Album Quilt Period. It is illustrated with 23 drawings carefully replicating original Baltimore Album Quilt blocks and one contemporary block. This Introduction develops the thesis that these Baltimore Album Quilts used symbolism *extensively* and often *intentionally*; that, in fact, these quilts "spoke without words."

When my husband and I were honeymooning in Germany some fourteen years ago, we had a gourmet treat the happy memory of which cheers us still. It was called *"Lied Ohne Worte"* ("Song Without Words") and was a sampler of the best dishes of Bavarian cuisine, artfully arranged on a large platter. The sensual pleasure of savoring each entree was augmented by our sense of self-indulgence. We could have it all!

The chef who named this offering "Song Without Words" understood well the appeal of so many good things in one spread. And it is just this appeal of a rich sampling which is echoed in the quiltmaker's love for the Album Quilt genre, a love now in its second century.

By the nineteenth century with well over one hundred years of traditional American quilt patterns behind them, quiltmakers turned with increasing frequency to combining different block designs in one quilt. When there are more dissimilar than similar blocks we call such quilts, broadly, Album Quilts.

In the Album Quilt, the ambitious quiltmaker, facing all the temptations of a burgeoning inheritance of quilt patterns, plus design ideas of her own, could indulge herself with a sampling in one spread. She, too, could "have it all."

But, like the Bavarian chef, the Album Quilt designer must present divergent parts as a melodious whole. She meets this challenge by a skillful harmonizing of color, design, setting, border, and binding. Having to surmount the difficulties of this design task may in fact contribute to the masterpiece quality of so many Album Quilts. For while a poorly conceived Album Quilt may have only fine stitches and sentiment to redeem it, an excellently conceived Album Quilt has an irrefutable elegance.

If an album is a "book for making a collection according to a theme," the term "Album Quilt" covers an entire classification of *theme* quilts. Within each quilt of the genre one finds the theme carried out through different designs, often symbolic; through different fabrics representing each maker; or through different inscriptions on each block.

GENA HOLLAND

The variety of Album Quilt themes is fascinating. Early in the nineteenth century master quiltmakers were already making "Legacy Quilts," each block a cherished pattern to be passed on. The quiltmakers who made "Sampler Quilts" vied to get as many varied designs as harmoniously as possible into one quilt. While a mother who made her son a "Freedom Quilt" did so for reasons of sentiment as well as artistry. Freedom quilts might be full of metaphoric designs and moral inscriptions, Mother's "last say" as it were. Presented to the young man when he came of age at 21, the quilt could then be put away to become his gift to his bride when he married.

While some Album Quilts were made by individuals, others were made by groups. Frequently the latter were "Presentation Quilts," testimonials to a minister or his wife, or a valued teacher or other public figure. There were "Friendship Quilts" made for a departing friend or as a token of affection and remembrance when an engagement was announced. A variation was the "Friendship Medley Quilt" in which friends made and signed blocks which were made of the same pattern but to which they had contributed different fabrics.

Album Quilts which were "Autograph Quilts" expanded the Victorian craze for autograph albums. "Family Autograph Quilts" might be made by one quiltmaker and signed by family members, or might be jointly made. A particularly interesting form of "Family Album Quilt" was the "Death Watch Quilt" in which each person sitting by the bedside of an ill and dying relative, made a square. In "Family Record Quilts" each block chronicled an important event.

The Victorians were demonstrative, in both their art and their written word, about their religious con-

SUSAN BRADSHAW   LORRAINE JACOBSON   JOANNE PARKS

victions, their moral beliefs, and their affectionate sentiments. "Scripture Quilts," "Bible Quilts," and "Quotation Quilts" all conveyed deeply held beliefs and fervent feelings in a literal way. In this, they were like the "Autograph Quilts" but the phrases carefully penned on them held to their more closely described purposes.

Even before the Victorian Period's passion for expressing religious, moral, and romantic sentiments explicitly in writing and implicitly through symbols, that most womanly Album Quilt of all, the "Bride's Quilt," had its own constellation of symbols: the rose, the heart, lovebirds and doves, linked rings.

Throughout quiltmaking history the Bride's Quilt was particularly important to American women. Its making was a rite whose precepts gave a tangible outlet to all the yearnings of a young woman for love and marriage, and to the heartfelt hopes of her friends and relatives that it be a fruitful match; one in which the couple's joys would outweigh their sorrows.

Bridal Quilt customs and styles varied. Elegant white on white quilts were the vogue for three quarters of a century until 1850, while the Double Wedding Ring pattern, popular since the late 1800s, remains a favorite today, though not necessarily as a Bride's Quilt. The "Rose of Sharon" appliqué pattern was a Bridal Quilt favorite of long duration and led the way for the "Appliqué Album Bridal Quilts." In these a lavish variety of appliqué designs were artfully combined, a very fashionable style by the mid-nineteenth century.

The most famous Appliquéd Album Quilts were those made in the Baltimore area in the 1840s and 1850s. The "Baltimore Album Quilts" were Presentation Quilts of all kinds, not Bridal alone. They gained a distinct name because of their superior artistry and because of the great numbers of such quilts produced in that particular time and place.

Intriguing speculation surrounds the makers of the Baltimore Album Quilts. Originally more of a group effort, there is strong evidence that individuals may have made some of the most impressive examples of the genre. The name Mary Evans (Ford) is connected with many quilts which seem to be made with the same artistic genius. In the pattern series which illustrates

this book, all the more realistic Victorian theme patterns (labeled Pattern Type III) might be credited to her hand except "Friendship's Offering" and "Hunting Scene." (More information on the patterns is found in the section About the Illustrations, following the Lexicon, and in the Pattern Notes opposite each picture.)

Specific blocks in many obviously group-made quilts have the same uniquely excellent draftsmanship, design, and execution. Did this "Mary Evans" design and sell patterns, or blocks, or do commissions, or participate in a sewing circle engaged in producing numbers of these Baltimore Album Quilts? Why were the best examples of this genre produced in such a brief period (1846–1852) of time? Such enigmas and more are the subject of the fascinating and thoroughly researched museum catalog, *Baltimore Album Quilts*, by Dena Katzenberg.

The Baltimore Museum of Art's Baltimore Album Quilt Exhibit toured the United States in 1981 and 1982. Its catalog reads almost as compellingly as a mystery story and contains a photographic gallery of the 24 Exhibit quilts. That display and book so caught American quiltmakers' imaginations that groups and individuals all over the country are now making Appliqué Album Quilts of their own.

My own enthusiasm for the genre led at first to recreating two dozen of the original Baltimore Album Quilt patterns. Undertaken in homage to the exceptional talent of those good ladies of Baltimore, reproducing the designs which now illustrate this book was a laborious task. It necessitated close study of the quilts pictured in the Baltimore Museum's catalog and elsewhere. I carefully tried to duplicate the shaded fabrics used to convey depth of form, the moiré prints which represented wood and mottled leaves, the inked-in details, the interior quilting, the expressively appropriate repliqué on floral forms.

As I worked I became convinced that the symbolism which is indigenous to American quiltmaking prevails in the Baltimore Album quilts. The text of *Spoken Without a Word* followed naturally. It is a small lexicon of symbols and their meanings and is illustrated with Baltimore Album Quilt Blocks. The search for meanings is inconclusive since I hesitate to impute specific intention to the use of symbolic

GENA HOLLAND

ROBYN MCKAY

MARVA GURLEY

imagery in the absence of convincing evidence. But consideration of the hypothesis is fascinating; it is a study in which the reader is invited to join.

Classic, Christian, Hebrew, Patriotic, and Floral iconographies were all familiar tongues to the Victorian ladies who made these quilts. My initial thought was that the same spirit of competition which drove them to heights of artistic excellence encouraged them to enrich their quilts with deeper meaning as well as overt sentiments. India ink which came into use in the mid-nineteenth century was used extensively on the quilt squares not only for sketches and fine detail (thorns, feathers, flower stamens), but also for inscriptions, verse, and scriptural quotations.

The written word is easier to decipher than symbolic tongues with which we are no longer very familiar. One clue pointing to significant meaning is repetition. For example, these blocks occur with notable frequency: Crossed Pine Cones—the pine cone signifying Life and Fruitfulness; Rings of Roses—the ring meaning Eternal, the rose connoting Love (or as a Crown of Roses the meaning implied is "Superior Merit"); and the Rose of Sharon—symbol of Romantic Love dating back to the initial reference to it in the Song of Solomon. It seems a reasonable assumption that if an image is used over and over again, and the usual meaning is consistent with the quilt's purpose, then symbolic interpretation is probably intended.

Religious representations recur at least as often as romantic ones. A common and elegant block depicts rosebuds (signifying purity) on the four sides of a squared wreath with a Fleur de Lis at each corner. The Fleur de Lis is a symbol for the Trinity and the Virgin Mary in Christian Iconography; and for the Flame of Light, Life, and power in the French national emblem. Spiritually significant grapes, cherries, and strawberries are the fruits most often featured as wreaths. The grape vine symbolizes Christ and the Church; cherry clusters denote Sweet Character and Good Works (cherry twins mean Love's Charm); a strawberry trefoil means the Christian Trinity, while strawberries in general are symbols for Esteem and Love, their leaves meaning Completion or Perfection.

To add a few additional often-used blocks, but by no means completing the list, there are crossed

oak branches, and oaks in wreaths and sprays, even acorns and oak leaves in a cornucopia! These mean respectively: Victory; Courage; Longevity, Immortality; the oak tree itself standing for Hospitality, Stability, Strength of Faith and Virtue; symbol of the Christian's Strength Against Adversity. Small wonder that with all these attributes the oak is also the state tree of Maryland, a state begun as a colony for persecuted Roman Catholics.

With properties of Triumph, Victory, Eternity, Success, Renown, Pride, and Good Fortune, the laurel crown or branch, symbolic since antiquity, is an obviously appropriate inclusion in a Presentation Quilt. The cornucopia is seen on quilts inscribed to both men and women. Connoting Abundance and Plenty it is sometimes filled with fruit, sometimes flowers, occasionally both. In the masterpiece quilt made for Captain George W. Russell of Baltimore in 1852, a Horn of Plenty graces each corner with unique touches which patently intend symbolic meaning. The Black-eyed Susan, State Flower of Maryland and uncommon in these quilts, is in the front center of one bouquet. A pineapple (for "You are Perfect" or Hospitality) perches atop another cornucopia otherwise full of flowers. A bird (denoting Life of the Soul) and butterfly (signifying Resurrection) are integrated into the third cornucopia's profusion of flowers, while the fourth is overflowing with fruits, but also includes a sprig of oak leaves and acorns whose symbolic meaning is Longevity. A lemon is placed prominently in the center of this last cornucopia and is a sign of Fidelity in Love, as well as the Harvest. The other fruits and their meanings include: an orange (Happiness, Prosperity), peaches (Salvation), two kinds of grapes (meaning, in general, the Blood of Christ in the Eucharist; wild grapes mean Charity), cherries (Sweet Character, Good Deeds), a sprig of unrecognizable berries, and an apple (symbol of Perpetual Concord, Salvation).

At least two Baltimore Album Quilt blocks feature the unlikely and difficult to present squirrel. He symbolizes Thriftiness, a virtue worth taking trouble over! Banners and banderoles, arrows, birds, books, butterflies, stars, palm fronds, cherubs, couples holding hands, stars, and lyres are all repeated design motifs

TERI A. YOUNG   CATHY GRAVES   NANCY CHESNEY-SMITH

with figurative meanings. That their usage is symbolic is sometimes confirmed within the quilts themselves. The lyre, Sacred Harp, or David's Harp each convey the meaning of All Music in Honor of God. Reiterating this intent we find these block inscriptions spelling out, quite literally, a similar motive:

> O may our hearts in tune be found
> Like David's harp of solemn sound
>
> Presented to Mrs. Lipscomb
> by Mrs. L. F. Michalson
> March 16th
> Baltimore 1847
> General Taylor Hero of
> Rio Grande

It seems clear that Mrs. Michalson, who presented this lyre block, wished to convey two important ideas: first, Christian devotion; and second, a tribute to Zachary Taylor, a contemporary patriotic hero.

The theme of Music in Honor of God is reiterated even more clearly in these three quotes from separate blocks in an anonymously made 1844–1845 Baltimore Album Quilt:

> With cheerful notes let all the earth
> To heaven their voices raise
> Let all, inspired with Godly mirth
> Sing solemn hymns of praise
>
> Oh for a thousand tongues to sing
> my dear Redeemer's praise
> The glories of my God & King,
> The triumph of His grace!
>
> Sing of the wonders of that love
> Which Gabriel plays on every chord
> From all below and all above
> Loud hallelujahs to the Lord

Books are recurring motifs. One is labeled "Friendship's Offering" and may be an autograph album, another "Sacred Melodies"; but most are labeled "Bible" and often have a person's name inscribed on the cover as well. The religious convictions inscribed on the quilts in the Baltimore Museum of Art's Exhibit are overwhelmingly Christian in tenor. This is important because it lends credence to the Christian symbolism interpretation of many of the design motifs. Two clarion examples are these two quotes. The first is from a ca. 1850 Baltimore Album Quilt made by the Ladies of the Caroline Street Methodist Church in Baltimore, and the second from a Baltimore Album Quilt made for The Reverend and Mrs. Robert M. Lipscomb in 1847:

> Why do we mourn departing friends?
> Or shake at deaths alarms?
> 'Tis but the voice that Jesus sends
> To call them to his arms.
>
> This Book
> This holy book on every line Mark'd with the seal
> of divinity: On every leaf bedew'd
> with drops of Love Devine, and with the
> eternal heraldy—And signature of God
> Almighty stamped from first to last,
> this ray of sacred light—
> This lamp, from off the everlasting
> throne, Mercy took down, and in the
> night of time stood, casting on the
> dark her gracious bow; and evermore
> beseech my men with tears, and
> earnest sights, to Read
> Believe, and Live.
> Accept this square affection brings
> tho' poor the offering be—
> It flows from Friendship's purest springs
> A tribute it is for thee
> To Rev. Robert Lipscomb
> Baltimore

CHERI LEFFLER

MARCIE LANE

At work here seems to be not so much a spirit of competition to enrich these blocks with meaning, but an ornate—by contemporary standards—mode of self-expression. It would indeed be very Victorian to compose a medley of symbols within their quilts: and so my hypothesis, that the Baltimore Album Quilts are laced with iconography.

But so many questions remain unanswered. What, for one, is the name of the pointed knit cap seen speared on many a flagstaff in the patriotic blocks? (See Pattern 6) Similar ones are seen on drawings of the mobs in the French Revolution. Can we surmise that this is a symbol of Francophilia, a reaffirmation of our nations' kindred zeal for Liberty, Equality, and Fraternity? What, then, is the cap's name and what is its exact meaning? What is the crested bird seen in so many of the blocks attributed to Mary Evans, and who can identify the many flowers with certainty? Because of so many open questions, I state my case for symbolism not as irrefutable fact, but as food for thought and earnestly invite the reader's contributions.

The information which exists on symbols used extensively by the Victorians is substantial. My excitement to share these thoughts and interpretations with you, my fellow quiltmakers, has produced this book. It is a compilation of selected symbols and their meanings, an introduction to symbolic design motifs from the Baltimore Album Quilt Period.

I am persuaded that the Baltimore Album Quilts were optimistic, benevolent gifts of respect, admiration, and love, and that they therefore contain symbols which are similarly positive. Where there was doubt as to whether a particular design motif was, in fact, represented in these quilts—a problem almost entirely of recognizing with certitude the various plants and flowers in their often highly stylized manifestations—I was guided by the above principal of benevolent intent.

"We live by Faith," Mary A. Haugh penned carefully in 1847 or 1848 (with never a splotch!) onto her block. Faith ruled my selection of which flowers to include in the Lexicon. If the symbolism were benevolent, that flower is included. If the sentiments implied seem inappropriate to a Bridal or Presentation quilt, that flower is omitted. Thus the yellow Chrysanthemum which means Slighted Love is missing.

If the sentiments seem inappropriate, yet the plant is clearly recognizable in a quilt, then that plant is included. The Fig, prominent on several quilts, means Lust. This from Adam and Eve's use to cover their nakedness in the Garden of Eden. Perplexing on a Victorian Bridal Quilt! However, further research shows a second meaning, Fertility from the Fig's many seeds. A much more likely intent!

Much of the resource material available emphasizes Christian symbolism. This is not inappropriate since research

ANNETTE E. JOHNSTON

indicates that many of these Quiltmakers were in Religious classes and church sewing groups together. The men's secret societies (Masons and Odd Fellows), whose symbols appear on some quilts, use Christian Iconographies predominantly.

This Wee Lexicon is an introduction, a beginning. I hope it furthers your acquaintance with the Baltimore Album Quilt genre—its symbols, meanings, and patterns. Hopefully, it will enrich your quiltmaking pleasure and induce you to create your own Appliqué Album Quilt, enriched by the memory of that Fascinating Lady, the Presentation Album Quilt of Nineteenth Century Baltimore.

Spoken Without a Word

A Lexicon of Symbols from the Baltimore Album Quilt Period

"The Flowers in silence seem to breathe
Such thoughts as language cannot tell."

DELIA P. KANE

THE COLLECTIVE BEAUTY OF the Baltimore Album Quilt is a Gift from another century. That gift as it stands is more than enough.

And yet—might there be more to it? The Ladies who made these quilts were Victorians. They were inhabitants of that rich time when Sentiment and Symbols threaded a ribbon of warmth and meaning through daily lives. They, after all, spoke the Language of Flowers.

We have some sense of that charming tongue. When he sends a red rose we know his love. But if it's yellow is he jealous? Ah, that is the question! Of course, we could err, and read too much meaning into the appliquéd garlands, the wreaths of grapes, the hummingbird's timeless hovering.

And yet—we are Quiltmakers too. A kindred sweet, shy passion inspires our works of artistry. A hint of who *we* are—and why—is allowed to show. Only the strongest of feelings impel a Masterpiece Quilt to completion. If we trust a person we'll share our intimate sentiments, and their secret symbols in our quilts. Even though those quilts' beauty is enough without additional meaning.

Has each Age its own shyness and its own outspoken certainties? What intrigues is that our very reserve may draw us to the Victorians' explicitness:

In all thy ways acknowledge Him and
he shall direct thy path.

Should I be parted far from thee,
Look at This and Think of Me.

May I twine a wreath for thee,
Sacred to love and memory.

These sentiments are carefully crow's quill-penned onto artful 1847–1850 Baltimore Album Quilt blocks: unabashed messages of Faith, Hope, and Love.

From out of a surpassingly graceful wreath of flowers on a 1846–1848 Baltimore Album Quilt block, we hear this bold call to the city's militia:

To the Gray Boys
Guardians of Freedom of
*   Justice and Virtue*
Citizens, Soldiers of Liberty's Soil
This token of friendship
*   I gladly present you,*
Then guard it from insult and
*   shield it from spoil*
Strong be the links in the
*   chain of your union*
And never the Soldier's proud
*   precept forsake;*
Long may you live in a
*   martial communion;*
And scorn'd be the slavery who
*   the compact would break.*

Proud Patriotic Sentiments! No querulous ambivalence here. And no deciphering is needed to read the civic pride. Baltimore's Washington Monument beams out from many a block in these Album Quilts, garlanded with floral beauty.

Symbols of the Space Age glint here and there in *our* quilts; the railroad, paddle-wheel steamer, merchant ships caught *those* quiltmakers' imaginations. For theirs was The Century of Progress, laurel-wreathed in its own time.

RITA VERROCA

Bright color, optimism, and signs of the Good Life entwine. There's a dapper sportsman duck hunting. And Mr. and Mrs. Sliver could afford to commission a breathlessly beautiful Bride's Quilt for their daughter Elizabeth in the year 1849.

Though from another century, so much is writ clear. But is there more? The women who made these quilts were devout, industrious, zealous, cultured, and full of feeling. Symbols were their dialect, motifs with larger meaning were their palette.

Yes, we risk imputing more than was intended. But where's the harm? Our love for the Baltimore Album Quilt is love at first sight. So let us consider the Victorian's Symbolic Tongue. We'll look afresh at those masterworks. To do so is to visit with the Good Ladies who gift us from the past, to try to become better acquainted with them, and to cherish them. And there can be no harm. For these Quilts' Beauty is more than enough.

The Lexicon of Symbols

A

Acacia Friendship, Platonic Love
Acacia, Rose or White Elegance
Acacia, Yellow Secret Love
Acanthus Leaves Admiring of the Fine Arts
Acalia Temperance
Acorn Longevity; Immortality
Agave Tree of Life, Abundance
Agrimony (of Rose Family) Thankfulness, Gratitude
All-Seeing Eye Omnipresence of God
Almond, Flowering Hope, Virginity and Fruitfulness, French Symbol of Happy Marriage
Almond Twins Lover's Charm, Symbol of Good Luck
Aloe Wisdom and Integrity (Greek)
Alyssum, Sweet Worth Beyond Beauty
Amaranth (Globe) Immortality; Undying Love; Faith, "My love will never fade or die!"
Amaryllis Pastoral Poetry, Splendid Beauty
Ambrosia Reciprocal Love
American Cowslip Heavenly Beauty
American Elm Patriotism
American Linden Marriage
American Starwort Hospitality, Cheerfulness in Old Age
Anchor Steadfastness, Safety, Protection, Salvation, Hope, The Soul
Angel Guardian, Protection
Apple Symbol of Perpetual Concord, Salvation (in Christ's hand) [Temptation (in Adam's hand), Sin]
Apple Bough Transport to Elyssium (Greek)
Apricot Blossom Shy Love
Arbor Vitae Tree of Life, Constant Friendship, "Live for me."
Arrow Romantic Love, Passion (Eros)
Arrows Dedication to the Service of God
Arrows, Bundle of Unity
Arum (Wake Robin) Ardor
Ash Tree Tree of Life, Grandeur
Aster Dainty, Elegant, Variety
Austertium Splendor
Azalea Restraint, Fragile, Temperance, Ephemeral Passion

RITA MACIONA

B

Bachelor's Buttons Celibacy
Balm Sympathy, Love, Pleasantry
Balm of Gilead Healing
Banner Victory. Victory over Death
Bay Tree Glory and Resurrection (Roman)
Bee Zealous and Industrious
Bee Orchis Industry
Beehive Industry, Unified Community, Strength in Unity
Beech Tree Prosperity
Begonia "Beware! I am fanciful!"
Bell Flower Fidelity
Bell Flower, (small, white) Gratitude
Betony Surprise
Birch Meekness, Light and Fertility
Birds In general, Life of the Soul (Christian)
Bittersweet; Nightshade Truth
Black Poplar Valor
Blue (Color) Truth (Christian)
Bluebell Delicacy, Constancy
Bonus Henricus Goodness
Book The Bible (Christian)
Borage Medieval Symbol of Courage
Bouquet of Full-Bloom Roses Token of Gratitude
Box Tree Firmness, Stoicism, Courage in Adversity
Branch of Currants "You please all."
Buckeye or Horse Chestnut Luxury, Good Health

Bundle of Reeds, with their Panicles Music
Bundle of Rods, or Fasces Union and Strength (Christian)
Butterfly Resurrection (Christian)
Butterfly Orchis Gaiety

C

Calla Lily Magnificent Beauty
Camelia, Red Unpretentious Excellence
Camelia, White Flawless Beauty
Carnation, White Pure and Ardent Love
Catchfly, Red Young Love
Cedar Strength
Cedar Leaf "I live for three."
Cedar of Lebanon Incorruptible, Noble
Celandine, Lesser Joys Yet to Come
Chains Symbol of the Passion, Salvation (Christian)
Cherries Sweet Character, Good Deeds
Cherry Twins Love's Charm, Good Luck Symbol
Cherub Protection, Presence of God
China Aster "I partake of your sentiments."
China Rose Ever Fresh Beauty
Chinese Chrysanthemum Cheerfulness under Adversity
Chrysanthemum, Red "I Love you."
Cinquefoil Maternal Affection
Clematis Mental Beauty
Clover Dignity
Clover, Four-Leaved "Be Mine."
Columbine, Red Anxious and Trembling
Coreopsis Always Cheerful
Coreopsis Arkansas Love at First Sight
Corn Productivity, Riches, Bread of Life
Corn Cockle Innocent Charm, Daintiness
Cornucopia Abundance
Cow Productivity
Cowslip Winning Grace
Cranberry Cure for Heartache
Crocus, Spring Young Joy
Crocus, Saffron Mirth
Crown of Laurel, Parsley or Pine Symbol of Victory
Crown of Roses Symbol of Superior Merit
Crown of Wild Olive Symbol of Victory
(Author's Note: Any of these "Crowns" may be read "Wreath of")
Currant "I am worthy of you!"

LYNNE HUNEAULT

D

Daffodil Regard; Annunciation, Easter

Daisy Innocence, Gentleness, Pure in Thought, Loyal in Love

Daisy, Domestic "I share your sentiments."

Daisy, Marguerite Love

Daisy, Multicolored Beauty

Damask Rose Brilliant Complexion, Ambassador of Love

Dandelion Oracle of Love and Time, "Faithful to you!"

Daphne Odora Gilding the Lily

Day Lily Motherhood

Dew Plan A Serenade

Dipsacus or Teasel "I thirst after you!"

Dittany of Crete Birth

Dittany, White Passion

Dog Fidelity, Trustworthiness, Watchfulness

Dog Rose "You have enchanted me!"

Dogwood Durability

Dove Innocence, Holy Spirit; Purity, Peace

Dove and Olive Branch Peace; symbol of a Rebecca, Oddfellow women's auxiliary

E

Eagle Courage, U.S. National Emblem; Generosity, Highest Inspiration; Resurrection

Edelweiss Daring, Honorable Courage

Eglantine Spring and Poetry

Elderberry Blossom Humility, Kindness, Compassion, Zeal

Everlasting Flower Attachment, Faithfulness, "Always Yours!," Remembrance

Everlasting Pea Enduring Pleasure

F

Fennel Worthy of all Praise, Strength

Fern Fascination

Fern, Flowering Reverie

Fig Fertility and Abundance (Hebrew); Argument, Lust (Christian)

Fig Tree Fruitfulness and Good Works, Peace (Hebrew)

Fir Tree Patience, Time, Fidelity, Boldness; Symbol of the Elect in Heaven (Christian)

Flag Patriotic Emblem

Flax Domestic Industry, Fate, "I feel your Kindness."

Fleur de Lis The Trinity, Heaven's Queen—The Virgin Mary (Flame of Light, Life and Power; National Emblem of France)

Flower-of-an-Hour Fragile Loveliness

Forget-Me-Not True Love; "Forget me not!"

Fountain of Water "Fountain of Health;" Associated with the Virgin Mary: "The Fountain of Living Waters." "For with thee is the Fountain of Life."

Fruit In general, a symbol of Productivity (Greek), Fruitfulness; May symbolize the twelve Fruits of the Spirit: Love, Joy, Peace, Long-suffering, Gentleness, Goodness, Faith, Meekness, Patience, Modesty, Temperance, and Chastity.

Fuchsia Amiability, Anxiety, and Trusting Love

Furze or Gorse Cheerfulness under Stress

G

Garden Chervil Sincerity

Garden Ranunculus "Your attractions are many!"

Garden Sage Esteem

Gardenia "I love you in secret."

Garland of Flowers Love's Bondage

Garland of Roses Virtue's Reward

Gavel Democratic Authority

Geranium, Oak Leaved Loyal Friendship

Geranium, Rose-Scented "I prefer."

Geranium, Scarlet Comfort

Gillyflower Affection's Ties

Gladiolus "You pierce my heart!"

Glory Flower Radiant Beauty

Goldenrod Treasure, Good Fortune

Goldfinch Savior Bird; Protection against Plague (Medieval); Eater of Thorns

GENA HOLLAND

Gooseberry Anticipation
Grain Productivity
Grape In general symbolizes the Blood of Christ in the Eucharest
Grape, Wild Charity
Green Leaves Hope Renewed

H

Hammer Joseph of Nazareth, Carpenter, also the Passion
Harp, Sacred Symbol of all Music in Honor of God
Hawk Divination
Hawthorn Sweet Hope, "You are my only Queen!"
Heart Charity; Love and Piety
Heart, Pierced Repentance; or Lovestruck; Heart Pierced by arrow
Hearts, Paired True Love
Heather, Purple Beauty in Solitude; Admiration
Heather, White Protection from Danger
Heliotrope Everlasting Love, Devotion
Hibiscus Delicate Beauty
Honesty or Satinflower "Money in all pockets"
Holly Christ's Crown of Thorns, also The Passion, Christmas; Foresight and Defence
Honey God and Ministry of Christ
Honeysuckle Devotion, Generous Affection, Mirth, Love's Bond. "We belong to one another."
Horn Symbol of Strength in Biblical Times
Hourglass Symbol of Life's Brevity
Hyacinth Peace of Mind, Prudence, Yearning for Heaven, Unobtrusive Loveliness

I

Iris Faith, Hope, Light, Wisdom, Valor, Promise, Message, Eloquence; Floral Emblem of the Virgin Mary, *Fleur de lis*
Ivy Matrimony, Fidelity, Eternal Friendship, Wedded Love

J

Jack-in-the-Pulpit Zeal, Ardor
Jasmine, Red Glee, "Our love will be intoxicating."
Jasmine, White Friendliness and Cheerfulness, "Our love will be sweet"
Jonquil Fierce Sympathy and Desire
Juniper Safety, Protection, Ingenuity, Initiative
Justicia Ideal Womanly Beauty

K

Kennedia Cerebral Beauty
Keys Security, Housekeeper, St. Peter
Keys, Crossed Keys to the Heart, Love

L

Lamb Innocence
Laurel Triumph, Victory, Eternity; Success and Renown; Pride and Good Fortune
Larkspur Ardent Attachment, Open Heart
Lavendar Loyalty, Constancy, Sweetness and Undying Love, "Fervent but silent love!"
Lemon Fidelity in Love; Symbol of Harvest (Hebrew)
Lemon Tree Discreet Passion
Lilac, Mauve "Do you still love me?"
Lilac, Purple Youthful Love
Lilac, White "My first dream of love!"
Lily, White Purity, Sweetness, Majesty, Sincerity, Immortality, Easter Flower, Flower of the Virgin Mary; Symbol of Motherhood (Semitic)
Lily-of-the-Valley Sweetness, Renewed Happiness, "Let us make up," Spring, Birth of Christ, Immortality, Tears of The Virgin Mary, Purity, Majesty
Linden or Lime Trees Conjugal Love, Marital Virtue
Liverwort Confidence
Locust Tree Elegance, Affection beyond the Grave
Lovebirds and Parakeets Love

M

Madonna Lily Resurrection and Annunciation, Easter, Virgin Mary
Magnolia Majestic Beauty and Sweetness, Love of Nature

Maidenhair Fern Secret Bond of Love

Mallow, Marsh Beneficence

Mandrake Conception and Fertility

Marjoram Blushes, Consolation, Gypsy Mascot
Flower for Lovers

Marsh Marigold Pensiveness, Winning Grace,
"You are my divinity!"

Meadow Lychnis Wit

Mignonette Beauty, Modesty, "Your qualities
surpass your charms."

Milkvetch "Your presence soothes me."

Mimosa Sensitiveness, Daintiness, "Be careful,
Do not hurt me."

Mint Virtue, Violent Love and Consolation

Mistletoe Love, Difficulties Overcome,
Affection, "I shall surmount difficulties,"
Magic Plant of the Druids

Monkshood Chivalry

Moss Maternal Love

Moss Rose Superiority, Pleasure

Mossy Saxifrage Affection

Mountain Ash Antidote and Mercy

Mudwort Tranquility

Mugwort Happiness

Mullein Medieval Herb of Love

Myrrh Joy

Myrtle Love, Sacred to Venus, Mirth, Joy,
Emblem of Marriage (Hebrew)

N

Narcissus Triumph of Divine Love and Eternal
Life over Sin and Death

Nasturtium Patriotism

Nightshade Truth

Nest, Bird's Refuge, Safety, Good Luck

O

Oak Branch Victory

Oak Leaves Courage

Oak Tree Hospitality, Stability, Strength of Faith
and Virtue; Symbol of Christian's Strength
Against Adversity.

Olive Peace

Olive Branch Safe Travel

One (number) Unity

Orange Happiness, Prosperity

Orange Blossom Purity, Virginity, Innocence
Symbol of Wedding, Fruitfulness, "I shall not
sin!"

BARBARA GEROW RUAULT

Osmunda Dreams

Ox Eye Daisy Patience, Flower of Midsummer
Day

P

Palms Achievement, Peace; Victory, Conquest,
Palm Sunday (Christian), Harvest (Hebrew)

Palm Tree Creative Power and Peace (Semitic),
Judea

Pansy Remembrance, Meditation

Parma Violet "Let me love you!"

Patience Dock Patience

Peach Salvation, Unequaled Charm

Peacock Immortality, (Legend has it that the
Peacock's body does not decay). The Hundred
Tail-Feather Eyes are the All-seeing Eyes of the
Church (Christian).

Pear Christ's Love for Man, Affection, Comfort

Peony Healing

Periwinkle Young Friendship

Persimmon Fond Remembrance

Peruvian Heliotrope Devotion

Pheasant's Eye Remembrance

Philodendron The Loving Tree

Phlox Proposal of Love; Sweet Dreams

Pine Cone Life, Fecundity (Semitic)

Pine Tree Fidelity, Boldness, Everlasting Life,
Stability, Venerability

Pineapple "You are perfect," Hospitality

Pink, Carnation A Woman's Love, Motherly
Love

Pink, Indian Double Eternal Beauty

Pink, Red, Double Pure and Ardent Love

Polyanthus Mysteries of the Heart

DELIA P. KANE

Pomegranate Life, Fertility
Poppy, Red Comfort
Poppy, Scarlet Grand Extravagance
Poppy, White Sleep Inducer
Primrose Early Youth, Young Love
Pussywillow Easter, Spring

Q R

Raven Solitude
Ring Never Ending, Eternal
Rose Love, Flower of Venus, Goddess of Love
Rose, Austrian "You are all that's Lovely."
Rose, Bridal Blissful Love
Rose, Burgundy Unconscious Beauty
Rose, Cabbage Love's Ambassador
Rose, Campion "Be worthy of my Love."
Rose, Damask Brilliant Complexion
Rose, Full Blown "I Love you."
Rose, Full Blown, over two Buds Secrecy
Rose, Maiden Blush "If you Love me, You will discover it."
Rose, Multiflora Grace
Rose, Musk American Beauty, Charming
Rose of Sharon Romantic Love, Linked with Love from the Song of Solomon
Rose, Single Simplicity
Rose, White Purity, "I am worthy of you."
Rosebud Beauty, Purity, Youth
Rosebud, White Maidenhood, Innocence
Rosebud, Moss "I confess my Love."
Rosemary Remembrance, Fidelity, Constancy

S

Sedum or Stonecrop Lover's Wreath
Shamrock Ireland, Light-Heartedness, Good Luck, Clover—Christian Trinity
Sheaf of Wheat Abundance
Shield Victory, Prowess in Battle
Ship Christianity, The Church
Snowdrop Hope, Consolation
Sorrel Affection
Southernwood Lover's Plant
Sparrow Symbol of the Lowly, Humble
Speedwell or Veronica Female Fidelity, Sanctity
Square, The Symbolizes the Earth, and Earthly Things while the Circle symbolizes Eternity
Squirrel Thriftiness
Star Divine Guidance (Christian)

Star, Five - Pointed Guiding Star of Nativity
Star, Six - Pointed Star of David, Star of Creation
Star of Bethlehem Purity, Reconciliation
Stock Lasting Beauty
Strawberry Esteem and Love, Intoxication and Delight
Strawberry Leaves Completion, Perfection
Strawberry Trefoil The Christian Trinity
Sunflower "My eyes see only you." Homage, Devotion
Swallow Summer, Incarnation, and Resurrection
Sweet Pea Delicate Pleasures, also Farewell
Sweet William Gallantry, Finesse, Flawlessness
Sycamore Fertility, Love

T

Tent Hospitality, Succor
Three Linked Chains Friendship, Truth, Love
Trillium Modest Beauty
Triple Love Knot, or True Love Knot Love
Trumpet History, Proclaim, Fame
Trumpet and Wreath Fame
Trumpet Flower Fame
Tulip Renown, Fame, Spring, Dreaminess
Tulip, Red "A declaration of love!"
Turtle Doves Purity, Sign of Mourning

U V

Violet Modesty, Simplicity, "I return your love."
Vine Christ, "The True Vine" in Christian Iconography; and also The Church where "God is Keeper of the Vineyard."
Vine, Wild Poetry and Imagination

W X Y Z

Wall Flower Constancy in Adversity
Water Lily Purity of Heart
Wheel Symbol of Divine Power
White Pink Talent
Willow, Water Freedom
Willow, Weeping Mourning
Willow Wreath Freedom
Wood Sorrel Joy, Motherly Love
Xeranthemum, or Eternal Flower Eternity and Immortality
Zinnia Thoughts of Absent Friends

About the Illustrations

THE TWENTY-FOUR BALTIMORE ALBUM Quilt block illustrations in this volume were selected primarily for use as patterns rather than primarily to illustrate the Lexicon of Symbols, though they do in fact show much symbolic imagery. Names have been given to the designs where no traditional name was to be found. They are labeled by pattern type according to these three design categories into which the Baltimore Album Quilt squares divide:

Pattern Type I: Patterns From Earlier American Tradition

Crossed Sprays, Wreaths, Pieced-Over-Paper Stars. All were older pattern formats which these Victorian Quiltmakers embellished with themes dear to their hearts.

Pattern Type II: Paper Folded Patterns

While paper folding is indigenous to American Appliqué Design, the Baltimore Album Quilt cutwork appliqué, cut from a single piece of folded cloth, has a special look. It resembles the "Scherenschnitte" dear to the Germans, many of whom settled in western Maryland. "Wheel of Hearts" is a full pattern showing German influence, while the frame on "Hunting Scene" and the basket in "Flower Basket" clearly are originally paper cuttings.

Pattern Type III: The More Realistic Victorian Theme Patterns

It is these patterns which give the exceptionally fine 1844–1856 Baltimore Album Quilts their unique appearance. Because these blocks, often pictorial, are ornate and

SYLVIA PICKELL

difficult to draft, more of them are included in this book.

The two dozen pictures in this volume are ready to use as thirteen inch block patterns. This size was chosen as the best uniform size for modern usage. For while the average quilt in the Baltimore Museum's Exhibit averages 100″ wide, some are huge by our standards. The largest is 127½″ × 142½″. Five blocks across, with or without sashings and borders, was the most common set. The blocks themselves thus tended to be large by comparison to contemporary styles. They ranged from 12″ to 18″; 16″ and 18″ being frequent sizes.

In the most common set, five blocks across, there are two rows of blocks bordering a center block of equal or enlarged size. The "Basket with Blooms, Bird, and Bible" is 18″ in the original attributed to Mary Evans. Surrounded by the "Garland Borders" it is a 36″ square, an enlarged central medallion (Pattern 11). The outer row blocks surrounding the original are 18″. The replicas in this Volume of these two

Please see page 57 for information on sizing patterns from this edition.

MARJORIE A. NELSON

patterns, block and border, are each 13″ and form a 26″ medallion.

The "Garland Borders" will fit any of the blocks pictured which have open corners, thus making them enlarged medallion centers. To use the "Garland Border" block with another block, simply line the side centers of the upper and left hand side of the center block with the bottom and right hand side of the "Garland Border" block. Repeat the border in this placement four times around the center block.

Another block designed as an enlarged central medallion is the "Butterfly Medallion" (Pattern 16) although when used as printed herein it can be a regular 13″ size block. Should you wish to enlarge or reduce these patterns you can do so right from this book by using an opaque projector with an enlarging or reducing lens. Or you can use a number of drafting techniques thoroughly described in Rita Weiss's book, *Artist's and Craftsman's Guide to Enlarging and Reducing Designs*.

A printer can enlarge or reduce the patterns by making photographic "stats." To go as high as 18″ he may have to shoot the design by halves for you to paste together. The best alternative is a photocopy place with a top of the line Xerox machine which copies up to 24″ or so in one step at less expense than a printer.

Bright, primary colors dominated the Baltimore Album Quilts. These were appliquéd in profusion onto neutral backgrounds: white, off-white, and sometimes tea-dyed fabrics. Turkey red and green are the most common colors used; turkey red is the most common border design and sashing color.

The illustrations in this book are shaded to show dark, medium, and light areas and as closely as possible to imitate the shaded fabrics and prints used. Good color photos can be found of these quilts in the quilt books listed in the Bibliography.

Solid color cottons formed the basic Baltimore Album Quilt palette. "Rainbow" or "Fondue" fabrics shaded from dark to light (sometimes in a moiré effect) give a light, graceful feel to some forms, and contour to others. The shaded screens illustrate this look effectively. You can imitate these shaded fabrics with paint or dye. Seminole stripping several shades from dark to light and back again will produce a similar looking cloth from which to cut your appliqué motifs.

Prints were used skillfully for special effects: circle prints formed a bird's eye, or were overlapped to form its talons or the twined effect of a harp's carved frame. Larger scrolled motifs imitated acanthus leaves framing an urn or cornucopia (see Pattern 2). The museum catalog, *Baltimore Album Quilts,* has a well-illustrated section on the prints which were unique to the Baltimore Album quilts.

How To Use the Patterns in this Book

TRACE OR PHOTOCOPY THE pattern from the book. For flawless, appliqué, transfer the whole block pattern to your 13″–13½″ square background fabric by tracing. Tracing onto paper or cloth (even dark cloth) is most easily done by using a light table. You can also next trace each unit for which you will need a template. When working on a very small scale you may find the simplest method for accuracy is English Paper Patchwork, in which case you'll want a lightweight paper pattern around which to baste the fabric for each piece of the design. A photocopy, cut up, would be quick and easy. Ironing your fabric pieces to freezer paper templates also works well.

For regular hand appliqué draw the shape of each design unit onto the right side of the appropriate fabric. This is your turning and sewing line. Cut out ¼″ beyond this pattern line. For machine appliqué cut out right on the line and satin stitch over the raw edge. It is important to note that when the hand done buttonhole stitching is used in the classic Baltimore Album Quilts both to appliqué and to emphasize an outline, it is usually done with sewing thread not embroidery floss, and is done over the regular fold line, not a raw edge.

Hand appliqué, using a fine Blind Stitch in the color of the uppermost fabric. Machine appliqué is not done on the original quilts but could appropriately be done today. A very fine satin stitch just a shade darker than the top fabric will blend into the motif and look at a short distance like fine hand work.

Of all the sewing on the Baltimore Album Quilts, the technique least visible in our present day repertoire is one for the extremely fine stems and the wicker in the baskets. Try this wasteful but wonderful method:

1. Iron a strip of bias in half. The wider it is, the easier it is to handle (2″ is ideal), you'll trim off the excess.

2. Trace the whole pattern, including the stem line, onto the background fabric for your block.

3. Baste the folded bias the length of the stem line with fold on left, raw edges on right. The distance from the fold to where you baste to the stem line is the width you want your stem. For hypothetical purposes we'll call it ⅛″.

4. Do tiny running stitches along the basted stem line from the top of the stem to the bottom.

5. Trim off all the excess from the raw edges (right side) to within ⅛″ from the line of running stitches.

6. Pull the folded bias from the left, across to the right, pulling it tightly against the running stitches which are now the stitches anchoring the left side of the stem.

7. Blind stitch the folded bias edge down the length of the right hand side of the stem, just covering the two trimmed raw edges. Sturdy slim ⅛″ stems are now at your fingertips!

DELIA P. KANE

KAREN MORAAL

LYNN SMITH

Embellishments of the *Baltimore Album Quilts* are a fascinating subject in themselves. A 1946 self-published book, *Old Quilts,* by William Rush Dunton is the classic work on Baltimore Album Quilts and describes the embellishments in minute detail, quilt by magnificent quilt, block by block. Suffice it to say that the Baltimore Album Quilt Period was a transitional period in which the block designs became more ornate, the symbolism became more profuse, and the embellishments became more intricate than those quilts which had come before. And subsequently, the symbolic motifs which adorned the Baltimore Album Quilts became the motifs which were painted, penned, and embroidered onto quilts of that late Victorian quilt genre, the Crazy Quilt; a quilt which depended for its very existence upon the needle art embroidery, which had been simply decorative in the Baltimore Album Quilts.

The Baltimore Album Quilts are the first genre to display much embroidered detail—in wool, silk and cotton. It may come as a relief to know that once in a rare while what photographs as an intricately serrated appliquéd leaf may in fact be a simple leaf shape with the serrations embroidered on! In addition to depicting fine detail, a common use of embroidery was outlining. The buttonhole stitch, outlining important shapes and wrought in a slightly darker shade than the object, was fairly common.

Water-fast brown India ink was a technological triumph of the mid-nineteenth century. It was used exuberantly on the Album Quilts for full sketches, inscriptions, and detailed embellishments. Examples of ink are shown in the patterns: thorns on stems, veins on leaves, stamens, etc. Ink is the predominant form of embellishment on the classic period Baltimore Album Quilts.

Other popular embellishments were padding—frequently with shapes and other berries, but also on roses—and quilting. Quilting was found on the interior of the appliqués themselves to define veins on leaves, or to puff a rose. Ruching, a gathering and puckering of material, was another technique used to create realism and three-dimensionality.

Postscript

AT FIRST GLANCE, THE blocks in the Baltimore Album Quilts are each different from the other. In fact, two, even four of the same type block often appear within one quilt. And variations on the same design appear repeatedly in separate quilts. When the blocks are clearly executed by different quiltmakers the resulting differences in style are fascinating.

In some cases the same design may have been repeated within a quilt for symmetry. In others these blocks may have been favored

MYRNA SHACKLETON

MARY FISCHEL

both for beauty and for particular significance. It strikes one, for example, that the religiously symbolic grape vine, anchor, and Fleur de Lis are executed over and over. One notes that wreaths come square, suggesting the Earth and Earthly Things, and circular suggesting Eternal Things. Even central Bow Knots on a Man's Presentation Quilt in 1852 are double looped, while the same exceedingly talented hand seems to have tied her Bridal Quilt garlands with a Triple Knot, the Lover's Knot. Intriguing indeed!

To what extent these quilts spoke symbolically—without words—remains a matter for conjecture. What is clear is that there was an evolution in a short period of time of a genre of Quilts which at first perfected variations on earlier American pattern traditions: crossed sprays, stars, wreaths. To this was added the unique influence of "Scherenschitten," that intricate paper cutting brought by Marylanders of German descent.

The crowning touch was the more realistic Victorian pictorial theme patterns. This Pattern Genre quite probably had earlier roots in the elaborate chintzes which were cut out and appliquéd *(Broderie Perse)* into quilt designs. Certainly themes of Trees of Life, Baskets, Cornucopias, Exotic Flora and Fauna are common to both. But these Victorian Quiltmakers in the excitement of their shared task and times, made the more realistic Pictorial Motif their own. And at its best, their

style, draftsmanship, and workmanship are breathtakingly superb.

The simply stylized flowers of Early American Patterns became elaborate *tours de force*. They reflect not only needlework and calligraphic accomplishment, but also the lush vegetation of Maryland's temperate climate. New England's Oak Leaves appear in the Quilts, but so does the magnificently decorative Fig Leaf. The shore-loving Trumpet Vine grows wildly around Baltimore, its brilliant orange blossoms luring the fragile Hummingbird as a daily visitor into the lives of the women who made these quilts. So the Hummingbird appears with as much frequency as the symbolic Dove and the exotic tropical birds of the chintzes.

It is in these Pictorial Blocks that we sense the joyous excitement of this period. The Good Ladies depicted modish glassware and basketry, Morocco-bound Bibles and beloved Albums (for "Friendship's Offering," or for poetry, or painted sketches—ladylike accomplishments of a peaceful time). Love of Life (and the Dead), love of Beauty, love for the one for whom the quilt is intended, love of their modernity and their traditions, their country, their technological progress—all are uninhibitedly reflected in these Victorian Theme Blocks with a verve that is infectious!

This, then, Gentle Reader, is your Heirloom Challenge: What do you so love from America's design heritage and your family's? What past patterns do you wish to cherish by reproducing them in your quilt? What so fires your imagination about the times in which you live? What progress are you thankful for? What in your garden and in your life warms your soul?

An Album Quilt is a happy thing, a loving thing, a beautiful thing. For a season or two or three of pleasure, embark on an Appliqué Album Quilt. The Gift will be to yourself, to those you love, and to our quilt-making heritage—a project of affirmation! What more can we ask from a humble bed cover than that it warm inside as well as out?

KATHRYN BERNSTEIN

Selected Bibliography

Bates, Virginia Church, *Needlework In America*, Viking Press, N. Y., 1979.

Bishop & Safanda, *America's Quilts And Coverlets*, E.P. Dutton, N.Y., 1972.

Burke, M.L., Ed. *The Language of The Flowers,* Price, Stern, Sloan, Los Angeles, 1965.

Dreyfus, Henry. *Symbol Sourcebook,* McGraw Hill, N.Y., 1972.

Dunton, William Rush, *Old Quilts,* Self-published, Catonsville, Md., 1946.

Furguson, George. *Signs and Symbols in Christian Art,* Oxford Univ. Press, N.Y. 1958.

Jablonski, Ramona, *The Paper Cut-Out Design Book,* Stemmer House, Owings Mills, Md., 1976.

Katzenberg, Dena S. *Baltimore Album Quilts,* The Baltimore Museum of Art, Baltimore, Md., 1981.

Lehner, Ernst. *The Picture Book of Symbols.* Wm. Penn Publishing Corp., N.Y. 1956.

Lehner, Ernst. *Symbols, Signs, and Signets,* The World Publishing Co., N.Y., 1950.

Lehner, Ernest and Johanna. *Folklore and Symbolism of Flowers, Plants, and Trees.* Tudor Publishing Co., N.Y. 1960.

Nelson, Cyril, Ed., *Quilt Engagement Calendar 1984,* E. P. Dutton, N.Y., 1984.

Orlofsky, Myron & Patsy, *Quilts In America,* McGraw Hill, N.Y., 1974.

Author's Note

IDEALLY, THIS WEE LEXICON will have piqued your interest. The volumes listed above have a wealth of information and hundreds of symbols which couldn't be included within the boundaries of the task set forth in the Introduction.

Documentation on the Floral meanings is best accomplished by the Bibliography. Meanings were virtually the same from source to source with paraphrasing back and forth.

The museum catalog, *Baltimore Album Quilts,* by Dena S. Katzenberg was invaluable for its historical research and for its Photographic Gallery of 24 Baltimore Album Quilts which allowed armchair investigations with a magnifying glass. Most of the quilts referred to, the appliqués illustrated, and the inscriptions quoted from blocks are in *Baltimore Album Quilts.*

An impressive selection of Baltimore Album Quilts is to be found in the out of print *Old Quilts,* by William Rush Denton as well. If you comb used book stores you may find a copy—grab it!

Spoken Without a Word Colophon

The illustrations for *Spoken Without a Word* were done by Elly Sienkiewicz on Aquabee Sketch Paper with Letraset printed screens. The typesetting was by Barbara Byrd of Dan Daniels Printing in Bethesda, Maryland. Baskerville type was used for the text, Quill for the titles. Book design was by Elly Sienkiewicz and Barbara Byrd.

The printing of the first edition is on 70# Scott Offset, Ivory. The cover stock is 65# Beckett Cover, Red, and the end papers are 70# Howard Felt Text, Razzle Red. The book was printed and saddle stitched by Dan Daniels Printing.

About the Author

ELLY SIENKIEWICZ IS OWNER of a Mail-Order Quilt Supply business, Cabin Fever Calicoes, which is where her quiltmaking passion has led in recent years. In the larger scheme of things she is wife of Stan, and mother of Donald, 12, Alex, 9, and Katya, 6. An artist and history teacher by training, she is also on leave of absence from an Independent Study Program for the Unitarian Ministry. In the midst of a hectic life, writing this small volume was a respite with the things she cherishes most: sense of family and one's bounty, the human saga and history, beauty, and the communion of quiltmaking.

Back Cover

This composite picture shows 18 of the patterns in this volume. In the typical classic Baltimore Album Quilt there would be another outer row of same size blocks. While this illustration does not represent a quilt *per se*, it will serve to show how the various patterns combine.

Enlargement Percentages for Larger Album Block Sizes

The patterns in this book are presented for an 8″ × 8″ finished block. If you prefer to make larger blocks and quilts in the classic Baltimore Album style, the simplest way is to use a photocopier to enlarge these blocks.

Current design area: 7¼″ maximum for an 8½″ square (includes ¼″ seam allowance all around) makes an 8″ block, finished. The 12½″ unfinished block size is that of the *Baltimore Beauties* series.

- **For a 10″ finished block,** enlarge 129% (9″ design area).
- **For a 12″ finished block,** enlarge 165% (11½″ design area).
- **For a 13″ finished block,** enlarge 179% (12½″ design area).
- **For a 14″ finished block,** enlarge 186% (13″ design area).
- **For an 18″ finished block,** enlarge 243% (17″ design area).
- **For a 22″ finished block,** enlarge 300% (21″ design area).

ROSALYNN MCKOWN

PHOTO: STEVIE VERROCA

Rita Verroca

PATTERN NOTES
Hunting Scene

This simple scene makes a charming block, enclosed as it is in the folded paper cut-out frame. Both the paper cut-out pattern designing technique and the simplified stolid figure show the German influence in the Baltimore Album Quilts. This bright red framed picture is in a fine quilt made in 1847–1850 and now in a private collection in Westminster, Maryland.

Pattern Type II

PHOTO: TERI A. YOUNG

Elly Sienkiewicz

Katherine Scott Hudgins Dunigan

PATTERN NOTES

Vase with Floral Bouquet, Harp, Doves, and Bible

This exacting design appears several times in the Baltimore Album Quilts and seems to be in the exceptional style credited to Mary Evans. The book is labeled "Bible" on its binding, and "Henry Wigart" (?) on the cover. The whole block has a bit of a funerary aspect to it and one wonders if the birds are mourning doves and the whole block done *in memoriam*. This pattern is taken from an 1848 Baltimore Album Quilt made for the Reverend Peter L. Wilson and is in the collection of the United Methodist Historical Society in the Lovely Lane Museum, Baltimore. Symbolic content is clearly intended in this block.

Pattern Type III

Barbara Dahl

Margaret Russell

Margaret Russell

Gena Holland

PATTERN NOTES
Heart-Shaped Garland

This elegant block is from a ca. 1849 Baltimore Album Quilt attributed to Mary Evans. The quilt is now in the Metropolitan Museum in New York.

Pattern Type III

PHOTO: TERI A. YOUNG

Dierdre Loughnane

PATTERN NOTES
Fleur de Lis and Rosebuds

Many renditions of this design are to be found in the Baltimore Album Quilts. This pattern is one of the most gracefully proportioned and is found in a quilt made for Miss Isabella Battee, ca. 1852. The quilt is in the Baltimore Museum of Art's collection. The Fleur de Lis and rosebuds are all Turkey Red in high contrast to the green leaves and wreath.

Pattern Type I

PHOTO: STEVIE VERROCA

Rosalind Wood
Thébaud

Rosalynn McKown

PATTERN NOTES
Lyre with Wreath and Bird

From a Baltimore Album Quilt made for Samuel Williams in 1846–1847, now in a private collection in Baltimore. This is a particularly graceful and well-proportioned example of the many Lyre blocks. One can see quite clearly the crested bird which is in so many of the blocks attributed to Mary Evans. Could it be a Cedar Waxwing? Or a Phoenix, symbol of immortality?

Pattern Type III

Ellen Heck

PHOTO: TERI A. YOUNG

Tresa Jones

PATTERN NOTES
Patriotic Block

Replete with symbolism, this block with flag and eagle motifs is the center equal-size square of an 1847–1850 quilt in a private collection in Westminster, Maryland. It is done in the style attributed to the elusive "Mary Evans" and was perhaps one of her earlier designs on a patriotic theme. There are several eagle blocks which are identical to each other and which appear to be improved upon, simplified versions of this one. They do not have the pointed cap ("Liberty Cap"?) nor the stars. An example of these "other eagle blocks" is on the cover of the 1984 Quilt Engagement Calendar, edited by Cyril Nelson. This version of the pattern is included because it does have the "Peasant's Cap" (?) seen in so many of the Baltimore Album Quilts.

Pattern Type III

Nadine Cassady

PHOTO: STEVIE VERROCA

PHOTO: TERI A. YOUNG

Jeanne Sullivan

Lynne Huneault

PATTERN NOTES
Friendship's Offering

Friendship's Offering (original name unknown) is a charming combination of Hearts, Flowers, Distelfinks, and Hummingbirds (?). The pierced heart connotes Lovestruck or Repentance. These hearts are the only ones to appear on the 1846–1847 Baltimore Album Quilt made for Samuel Williams. The block is inscribed "Lizzie Morrison" and any conjecture about her relationship to Mr. Williams is left to the symbol-sleuthing of the reader. The quilt is now in a private collection in Baltimore.

Pattern Type III

PHOTO: STEVIE VERROCA

Rita Verroca

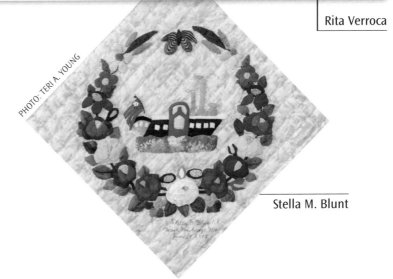

PHOTO: TERI A. YOUNG

Stella M. Blunt

PATTERN NOTES

The Steamship Captain Russell

Many examples of "modern technology" are shown in the Baltimore Album Quilts. In this case it is the steamship, named after Captain Russell for whom this Presentation Quilt was made in 1852.

Pattern Type III

Mary K. Tozer

PATTERN NOTES

Acanthus Leaves with Hearts and Arrows

This block design is a unique version of an exceptionally common Baltimore Album Quilt design. It is from an 1850 Baltimore Album Quilt in a private collection. Within the same quilt is the usual rendering of this pattern: Acanthus leaves with the tall spiked Acanthus bloom in red. In other versions the flower has two stylized bracts growing at the base of the bloom. An Ionic scroll is the pedestal for each plant and would seem to augment the Acanthus leaves' symbolic meaning: Admiring of the Fine Arts. A colored picture of both versions of this pattern is in the *1984 Quilt Engagement Calendar*. Though rare, this version with hearts and arrows (and romantic implications!) is so charming that it is the pattern included here.

Pattern Type I

Marie E. Collins

PHOTO: PEPITO MASTERPIECE PORTRAITS

Rosalynn McKown

Carolyn Goff Kimble

PHOTO: TERI A. YOUNG

PATTERN NOTES
Basket with Blooms, Bird, and Bible

This is the central motif of the enlarged center medallion of an elegant quilt inscribed: "To Miss Elizabeth Sliver/ This is/ Affections tribute Offering/ Presented by Father and Mother/ to/ Miss Elizabeth Sliver/ Baltimore - 1849." The design style is that traditionally attributed to Mary Evans. In the original (now in the Baltimore Museum of Art) this basket (18") is surrounded by the "Triple-Bowed Garland Borders," shown on the following page, to form a 36" medallion.

Pattern Type III

Delia P. Kane

PATTERN NOTES
Triple-Bowed Garland Borders

These are the garlands which, when repeated four times, surround the Basket Block on the preceding page to make the enlarged center medallion. In this pattern series' 13″ scale, the Basket plus Borders form a 26″ medallion. To form the 36″ medallion of the original quilt, enlarge this and the preceding pattern by 50% of the design image area only. This design image is 12″, so 50% will bring it up to 18″ and with the center block also increased to 18″ your medallion will be 36″.

These Garland Borders can be used with any open cornered block in this book. Simply match the side centers of the pattern you've chosen with the dotted lines on the border block to create your own patterns.

Pattern Type III

Janet Zehr Esch

Janet Zehr Esch

PATTERN NOTES
Central Medallion

This is from a quilt commissioned by the Sliver Family of Baltimore in 1849 for their daughter, Elizabeth. The quilt is now in the Baltimore Museum of Arts Collection. The illustration shows the set of the preceding block and border patterns.

Pattern Type III

Evelyn Crovo-Hall

Karen Pessia

PATTERN NOTES

Heart Wreathed with Vine

This pattern was drafted from the best of several examples of this design. It is from the 1847–1848 Baltimore Album Quilt made for the Reverend Dr. George C. M. Roberts. This quilt is now in the collection of the United Methodist Historical Society, Lovely Lane Museum, Baltimore. This is a sophisticated design which appears simple because its axial symmetry is so carefully worked out. It seems to come directly from the paper-cut Valentine tradition so in vogue in the mid-nineteenth century. If one were to interpret this block symbolically the heart can represent Piety, Devotion to Christ, "The True Vine," and The Church, where "God is the Keeper of the Vineyard." Another version of this pattern has crossed keys (Keys to the Heart, Love) in the center and doves beneath the heart, conveying a more romantic meaning. Understandably a popular pattern, there are several more examples of it in Dunton's *Old Quilts*. One of these hearts is wreathed in rosebuds, another in a cherry garland—clearly Love is the theme here!

Pattern Type II

Mary K. Tozer

PHOTO: TERI A. YOUNG

Part II: 1983 Edition　**83**

Mary Cargill

Kathryn Tennyson

PATTERN NOTES
Herald Angels

One of the Victorian pictorial theme blocks, this one is inscribed "To Rev. Robert Lipscomb/ 1847/ 'Behold, I bring you good tidings'/ of great joy, which shall be to all people/ Luke 2nd Chap. Verse 10th." This square is from a quilt made for the Reverend and Mrs. Robert M. Lipscomb now in the collection of the United Methodist Historical Society, Lovely Lane Museum, Baltimore. The original is approximately 15″ square. In this 13″ pattern the angels have been simplified slightly. This is a unique design not seen elsewhere.

Pattern Type III

Madeline Swope

PATTERN NOTES
Pineapples

Pineapples appear repeatedly in the Baltimore Album Quilts. This pattern is from a Baltimore Album Quilt made for Samuel Williams in 1846–1847, now privately owned. Long in American tradition as a symbol of Hospitality, the pineapple also connotes the romantic conviction: "You are perfect." This pattern's simplicity makes it an excellent foil for some of the more ornate Album Quilt blocks.

Pattern Type I

Rita Maciona

Sandra Rochon

PATTERN NOTES

Trumpet Vine

This is a pattern seen in several variations, with no traditional name to be found. Perhaps it is indeed the deep-throated trumpet vine flower with complex leaves which is one of Maryland's loveliest natural beauties. This pattern's origin must have been the silhouette paper-cutting, or "Scherenschnitte." There are to be found in the Baltimore Album Quilts a whole group of patterns based on a central square like this (sometimes on the diagonal) with very formally stylized flowers—often in urns—pointing out to each of the four corners. This challenging pattern is from an 1847 Baltimore Album Quilt made for the Reverend and Mrs. Robert Lipscomb and now in the possession of the United Methodist Historical Society, Lovely Lane Museum, Baltimore.

Pattern Type II

Rita Verroca

Bette F. Augustine

PATTERN NOTES
Butterfly Medallion Center

This block is designed to be the enlarged center square of an Appliqué Album Quilt. Presented here in uniform block size, it can be enlarged if the reader chooses to use it as a center medallion. The pattern is a contemporary original designed by Eileen Hamilton-Wigner in 1983. One wishes there were more Album Quilt block designs forthcoming from this exceptionally talented hand.

Contemporary Pattern Type

Honoring Bette Florette Augustine
Administrator, Emeritus, The Elly Sienkiewicz Appliqué Academy

Serendipity brought Bette, as Administrator, to The Elly Sienkiewicz Appliqué Academy 16 years or so ago. So many, myself included, found a haven in this 1995–2014 conference under Bette's care. Academy's blossom opened wider, smiled—more brightly; we teachers worked our hardest; volunteer staff could not have more devoted themselves to attendee happiness. Bette, born a leader, has the perfect touch: clear-thinking, humored firmness, concern for all those in her care. Bette's artistry, like her caring, became her trademark.

Only in more recent years, with the modesty that is her charm, had assembled Academicians been able to share Bette's miniature stitcheries, exquisite treasures! When I noted, "*SWAW* has no model for my mother's butterfly!" Bette, as so often, quickly volunteered. She explains, "I am a block maker! What freedom I found once I understood that liberating phrase. It was then I began my real adventures in appliqué." Of appliqué, Bette has said it transformed her, as though an emerging butterfly, "offering ever-renewing stimulation and joy." It is a privilege to love and honor Bette here.

PHOTO: TERI A. YOUNG

Patricia Hansen

PATTERN NOTES
Grape Vine Wreath

This pattern is from a Baltimore Album Quilt ca. 1843–1845 in a private collection. There were a great many grape vines, sprays, and clusters in the Baltimore Album Quilts. This pattern, from an early quilt of the genre, has a tight rhythm to it, a look which relaxed and became more irregular in the later 1846–1852 Baltimore Album Quilts.

Pattern Type I

PHOTO: CANDACE SHOEMAKER

Yolanda (Yoly)
Tovar

PHOTO: TERI A. YOUNG

Dawn Wakelam Hunt

PATTERN NOTES

Strawberry Clusters in the Shape of a Cross within a Circle

This is an ornate strawberry wreath from a ca. 1847–1850 Baltimore Album Quilt in the collection of the Baltimore Museum of Art. The strawberry leaves stand for Completion/ Perfection, the Cross for Salvation, the circle or ring for Eternity. Variations of the strawberry wreath are common in the Baltimore Album Quilts.

Pattern Type I

PHOTO: TERI A. YOUNG

Mary Ann Bloom

Robby Wargny

Elly Sienkiewicz

PATTERN NOTES

Flower Basket

This basket is particularly charming with its simple floral arrangement. The basket is undeniably Victorian in style but must owe its drafting to the paper-cutting technique. Two acorns connoting Longevity and Immortality are tucked in between the stems undoubtedly to give more weight to both the design and the symbolic significance of this block. The square is from a rich and lively quilt made for the Reverend Dr. George C. M. Roberts in 1847–1848 and is in the Lovely Lane Museum of the United Methodist Historical Society in Baltimore.

Pattern Type II

Karen Pessia

PATTERN NOTES

Eight Pointed Star with Sprigs of Berries

Stars appeared throughout the Baltimore Album Quilts. This is a unique pattern example of great charm and comes from an 1847–1848 Baltimore Album Quilt made for the Reverend Dr. George C. M. Roberts. The star means everywhere the same: Divine Guidance.

Pattern Type I

Ardie Sveadas

Ann Rust

PATTERN NOTES
Washington Monument in Baltimore

Many public buildings and monuments were depicted in the Baltimore Album Quilts and the Washington Monument was a favorite. For a spectacular series of four "Building Blocks" used to form an enlarged center medallion, see *America's Quilts and Coverlets* by Bishop and Safanda. This monument block is taken from a Baltimore Album Quilt made for Miss Isabella Battee ca. 1852, now in the collection of the Baltimore Museum of Art. The reader may wish to use the well-designed lyre-shaped wreath, if not the whole monument block pattern.

Pattern Type II

Anne Barney

PHOTO: JEFFREY LOMICKA

Karen Pessia

PATTERN NOTES

Cornucopia with Fruits and Acorns

Cornucopias, symbols of Abundance, were plentiful in the Baltimore Album Quilts. They must be difficult to draft, however, for many of them are rather ungraceful. This example from a man's Presentation Quilt, one made for Captain George W. Russell in 1852, seems particularly well done. The original quilt, done all in the style connected with Mary Evans, is in the Baltimore Museum of Art's Collection.

Pattern Type III

PHOTO: ROLAND DORSAY

Joan Dorsay

Elly Sienkiewicz

PATTERN NOTES

The Rose of Sharon

Variations of this earlier American Appliqué Bridal Quilt favorite appear repeatedly in the Baltimore Album Quilts. A precise symmetrical version is presented here from an early 1843–1845 quilt in a private collection. When this design appears in slightly later Baltimore Album Quilts it is loosened a bit by a softer, slightly asymmetrical arrangement of buds and leaves.

Pattern Type I

Carolyn Goff Kimble

Susan Prioleau

PATTERN NOTES
Wheel of Hearts

This striking and strong design forms the center block of a quilt made for George Holtzman ca 1847–1849, now in the Baltimore Museum of Art's Collection. The pattern shows the German "Scherenschnitte" (papercutting) influence. It is bold in concept and bold in color, being a solid turkey red whole cloth cutout. Dena Katzenberg, in *Baltimore Album Quilts,* notes that George Hotzman is referred to frequently as a teacher of Religious classes in the Methodist Church. If this block were made or commissioned by a grateful student, then this symbolic interpretation would make sense: The hearts denote Charity, Love, Piety, and are integral with the wheel which symbolizes Divine Power. This center block is of equal size (approx. 12″) to the other 24 blocks in the quilt.

Pattern Type II

Edie Zakem

Building Blocks for Baltimore's Album Monument

Barbara Dahl

Dr. Dunton, Mary Evans, and the Baltimore Album Quilt Attributions

When I first wrote *SWAW1983*, I had appliquéd, but it had been with the time-consuming preparation I'd learned as a child. I came to doubt that one person could have designed, stitched, and finished so many quilts in so little time. If I were then the proficient "appliqué-er" so many of us have now become, I might never have gotten so caught up in testing Ms. Katzenberg's single-artist attribution theory. But I did and presented a rebuttal at the American Quilt Study Group annual meeting, Bethesda, Maryland, October 1989. It was published as "The Marketing of Mary Evans" in the group's journal *Uncoverings* for that year, and excerpted in *The Magazine Antiques,* 1990; then presented by invitation at The Smithsonian Institution the same year and published, 1991, as "Dr. Dunton, Mary Evans, and the Baltimore Album Attributions," in *Baltimore Beauties and Beyond, Volume II.* Now an original source element in the Revivalist Albums' story, it follows.

IN OUR JOURNEYS TOGETHER, we have already touched on diverse potential influences on the Album Quilts. My intent has been to suggest new ways of looking at these quilts. Thus, ideally, two classic books in the field should also be read: William Dunton's *Old Quilts* and Dena Katzenberg's museum catalog, *Baltimore Album Quilts.* Everyone who becomes deeply involved in studying and writing about these quilts brings a certain mind-set and vision to them, a certain body of knowledge and research interests, and yes, certain artistic preferences. Only multiple voices will help us fully appreciate and understand the Album Quilt genre in all its diversity. And no single explanation can enlighten us fully on so complex and widespread a cultural phenomenon as these mid-nineteenth-century Album Quilts.

When Volume I was written in 1988, it seemed impossible to write about Baltimore Album Quilts without considering Mary Evans. Dena Katzenberg in Baltimore Album Quilts attributes numbers of these quilts to this woman about whom so little, really, is known. The feeling growing among many contemporary Album Quilt makers was that no one person, alone, could have worked so fast, with such diversity of design and with such intricacies of embellishment, and at such a sustained pace as to have created so many masterpieces in a short period of time. My fascination with the question of her authorship consumed the early half of 1989. And because the Mary Evans theory has caught the imaginations of so many, it seems important to share something of that winter's work here.[1]

First, who was Dr. Dunton and how is he connected to the Mary Evans attribution? Dr. William Rush Dunton, Jr. (1868–1966), whose unpublished *Notebooks* are the original source for the name Mary Evans (married name, Ford), was an Album Quilt scholar. *The National Cyclopedia of American Biography* devotes a half-page to Dr. Dunton, highlighting his role as a psychiatrist and one of the founding fathers of occupational therapy. Only a few lines in that biography hint at his love for needlework and quilts. One such clue is his belief that quiltmaking would restore a positive state of mind to "nervous ladies"; another, the fact that one of his contributions to medicine was the introduction of "white duck" fabric for use in interns' uniforms; and

DR. DUNTON

finally, the inclusion of the phrase "old quilts" in a list of his hobbies. By contrast, it is delightfully clear from the record he left behind that Dr. Dunton's quilt hobby was nothing less than an abiding passion and it is this "quilt record" which is of particular interest to us as quiltmakers.

Dr. Dunton felt the data he had researched and collected on the old quilts of Maryland and surrounding regions was so important that he self-published 2,000 copies of *Old Quilts* in 1946. Now a rare collector's item, that book was the first study to include in detail what we now call, loosely, the Baltimore Album Quilts. In addition to *Old Quilts*, Dunton left files, over a dozen "notebooks" (scrapbook albums, correspondence, news clippings, articles written by him, photos), and a partial manuscript for a book in progress, a "Dictionary of Quilt Names and Patterns." Now collectively called the William Rush Dunton, Jr., *Notebooks*, and housed in the Baltimore Museum of Art, these uncataloged papers are a treasure trove of quilt history. Dunton corresponded with such quilt luminaries as Marie Webster, Florence Peto, Carlie Sexton, Phoebe Edwards, and many others, whose names are no longer familiar to most of us. Included are Dunton's letters to batting companies, bed manufacturers, and an indelible ink company—all seeking answers to questions raised by these old quilts.

Perhaps Dunton discussed authorship of the Baltimore Album Quilts with Florence Peto, for in her 1939 book she wrote, "One wonders if there might not have been professional needlewomen in Baltimore and possibly other localities who specialized in fine quilts and spreads for bridal trousseau. There seems little evidence to support my idea except the character of the workmanship on the quilts." Dr. Dunton was still pondering the same question when he published his book in 1946.[2]

"I have a theory which cannot be proved," wrote the psychiatrist cum quilt expert in *Old Quilts*. "An artist . . . made her living by making [Baltimore Album] quilts . . . [and she] acquired considerable local fame." This modest statement doesn't sound like the stuff of which myths are made, but it may have happened. Mary who? Fewer people would ask that question in 1989 than in 1988, for the answer had been streamlined and packaged for popular consumption. Two books published in 1974 first tentatively suggested that Mary Evans might be just that needleartist whom Dr. Dunton sought. Fifteen years later, cautious speculation had given way to confident assertion. The word was out. Mary Evans was a "master quiltmaker," the "first professional quiltmaker."[3] Mary Evans supplied "prefabricated blocks for which she received payment" and signed "those blocks in a standardized script with their donors' names."[4] Mary Evans seemed to be the hottest-selling quiltmaker of the mid-nineteenth century. Is it true? Did she really make—in roughly a half-dozen years—the more than a dozen quilts now popularly attributed to her? Let's look at how that assumption may have affected quilt prices in recent years.

Record quilt prices of six years ago look like bargains today as Americana prices escalate. On January 21, 1989, a Baltimore Album Quilt dated 1850 and described as "the work of Mary Evans . . . commissioned as a gift for Mary Updegraf by her wealthy family"[5] sold at Christie's Auction House in New York for $132,000. (The same quilt appeared on the cover of Dutton's Quilt Engagement Calendar 1984.) Thomas K. Woodard (owner of Thomas K. Woodard: American Antiques and Quilts) told me that it had sold at the time of that publication for $26,000, so the 1989 sale shows more than a five-fold increase in just five years. At Sotheby's January 1987 Americana auction, another classic Baltimore Album Quilt sold for $176,000, and, according to its buyer, Frank J. Miele of Hirschl & Adler Folk, resold the same evening for "at least $200,000." In 1988, a classic Baltimore Album Quilt dated 1848 and inscribed "To John and Rebecca Chamberlain," with the maker listed as "probably Mary Evans"[6] sold for $110,000. In 1972, the National Antiques Review had pictured that same quilt and reported that at the Pennypacker Auction House in Kenhorst, Pennsylvania, "it surpassed everything else in beauty, interest, and price—$3,800."[7] In sixteen years, then, this classic Baltimore Album Quilt had increased in price roughly 3,000%.

January 21, 1989, was a Saturday quilt shoppers will remember. It was fur weather and antiques were in the air. Those who made the Christie's/Sotheby's/Winter/Antiques Show[8] circuit quickly caught a theme: all three were offering Baltimore Album Quilts attributed to Mary Evans. "It's her! It's another quilt by Mary Evans!" I heard exclaimed for the third time. I had been standing awhile at the top of Sotheby's main staircase, making notes on the quilt "attributed to Mary Evans, Baltimore, Maryland, mid-19th Century."[9] When the young man added, "It's not as nice as the one that sold at Christie's this morning," I couldn't refrain from asking what the quilt at Christie's was like. He and his friend shared their catalog. "And the one at the Winter Antiques Show?" I asked. "Oh, it was much fancier than this one, but here, take this extra ticket, we have to catch our plane." I had a train to catch, too, but there would be other trains.

My stopover at the Winter Antiques Show was worth it. I recognized the quilt in America Hurrah's booth from the *Quilt Engagement Calendar 1989*, where its caption reads: "inscribed Ellenor [sic] and Elizabeth A. Gorsuch, ca. 1840 . . . many blocks . . . may confidently be attributed to the hand of Mary Evans." (Birth dates for Mary Evans are given variously as 1829 or 1830, making her ten or eleven years old in 1840. It is hard to imagine so young a child having made a piece of needleart of this magnitude.) The Gorsuch Album Quilt was labeled at the show as having descended in a Baltimore County family with the date now changed to "circa 1845." Such provenance alone makes it very valuable even without further specific attribution. "Sold," proprietor Joel Kopp replied to my fellow customer's query, "for a high five-figure price."

The three Baltimore Album Quilts offered that Saturday had all been advertised in print as "attributed to Mary Evans" or "made by Mary Evans"— yet her name appeared on none of them. What is the origin of this attribution? The name "Mary Evans" was connected to the Baltimore Album Quilts in the mid-twentieth century by quilt expert Dr. Dunton with his "theory which cannot be proved," and despite subsequent research, it remains unproven today. Her name doesn't appear on any Baltimore Album Quilts that we know of, yet this attribution to Mary Evans, is confidently asserted in the market-ing of these quilts. Thus, while the popularity of quilts as collectors' items is now well established, quilt authentication standards in the marketplace need to catch up.

Attribution to Mary Evans (for one unappliquéd block only) seems to have begun with a manuscript dated 1938 in the Dunton Notebooks. In 1974, Patsy and Myron Orlofsky[10] and Marilyn Bordes[11] published the first tentative references to Mary Evans by name. They cite (either in person or in print) the Dunton Notebooks as their source. I went to the Baltimore Museum of Art to read for myself the reference to Mary Evans in these fragile old documents. The Notebooks convey in Volume VIII that Evans Bramble (identified by Dena Katzenberg in Baltimore Album Quilts as Arthur Evans Bramble, Mary Evans's great-nephew) brought Dr. Dunton a set of seven quilt blocks.[12] One, a central medallion block depicting the City Springs, Dunton records through a photograph and a notation as "made by Miss Ford" (Mary Evans's married name). That attribution is contained in a

GENA HOLLAND

seven-page description of this set of blocks. The sophisticated City Springs block, which is only basted, is in the very realistic, decorative, Victorian-style uniquely associated with Baltimore. By virtue of its being connected to Mary Evans through the *Notebooks,* this block's style, one that weaves through the Baltimore Album Quilts, has come increasingly to be thought of as Mary Evans's style.

If made during the heyday of the Baltimore Album Quilts, that City Springs block would have been begun one hundred or so years before being brought to Dr. Dunton. We won't ever know exactly what phrasing Mr. Bramble used to attribute this work to his great-aunt, but the passing of some one hundred years, one suspects, might cloud the Evanses' recollection of exactly what Great-Aunt Mary's role in that block had been. Did Mary Evans design the elegant City Springs block herself? Or did she cut it out of fabric from someone else's design? Was it her own work in this block at all, or had someone else cut and basted the motifs for Mary Evans to finish?[13]

Some of the other blocks in the set are already signed, though none "Mary Evans," and the needlework, in Dunton's words, varies in quality from "quite beautiful" to "rather crude." Might this have been a group-made

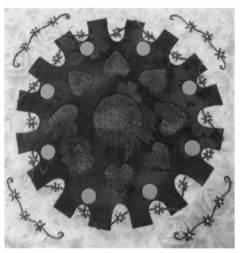

KATHERINE SCOTT HUDGINS DUNIGAN

presentation quilt with young Mary helping with the sewing? Or had these blocks come in from friends as contributions to Mary's own, never finished, Album Quilt? Was she, in fact, a professional seamstress or simply the designated sewer who had been brought the basted center block to appliqué and the other blocks to set together when all were finished? In any one of these suggested roles, the block connected to her might have descended in her family as "the work of" Great-Aunt Mary. In the end, while the City Springs block does clearly reflect a design style, we don't know for sure whether this style is Mary Evans's or that of another. And if it is Mary Evans's, we don't know whether she originated the style or was one of a number of people working in that style. This block was brought to Dunton with two completed quilts, both rather mundane square-patch variations. We are not told if they, too, were the work of Mr. Bramble's great-aunt, Mary Evans. What can safely be said is that, photographed in black and white, at least, they don't show the distinctive spark of an artist.

Katzenberg gives the birth/death dates for Mary Evans as 1829–1916 and cites the services in her book of Robert Barnes, genealogist. Dunton records what are presumably Evans Bramble's dates for Mary of 1830–1928. If Katzenberg is right, then Great-nephew Bramble is wrong at least on this item in his facts about the block and its maker. One must also question why, if Mary were either an extraordinary needleartist or a prolific professional quiltmaker, her family seems to have had so little evidence about her quiltmaking activities. Mary Evans lived to be 87 years old, by Katzenberg's dates, or 98 years old, by Evans Bramble's dates. By both reckonings, she lived right

into those early twentieth-century decades when Dunton himself was actively researching quilts. Yet seemingly the only evidence of quiltmaking activity to come out of all those years of adult life is one unfinished block said to have been begun when she was 20.

While he records this block as made by "Miss Ford," William Dunton does not once suggest that she might be "the artist" whom he seeks as the maker of other Baltimore Album Quilts. In writing about this set of blocks, he does reiterate his alternative theory that there may have been shops which sold patterns for these unusual designs. And what of Dunton's opinion of the possibility that Mary Evans may have been the artist in his theory? After having written about this "entertaining" set of blocks and Miss Ford in 1938, he left them and her out completely when, eight years later in 1946, he published his magnum opus, *Old Quilts*. Then again when, towards the end of his life, he compiled the files which "should go with the albums to the Baltimore Museum of Art . . . where [they] will be accessible to anyone who may be interested," he makes no mention of Mary Evans in all of his alphabetized letter-file boxes. He does, however, refer back once in those files to the City Springs block, though with no attribution to Mary Evans. In the manuscript section on naturalistic appliqué, for his never-published quilt dictionary, he wrote, "There was also a large block made for a quilt which was never completed which showed a familiar sheltering, one of the City Springs. Unfortunately during the absence of the owners, their house was broken into and this fine piece has been lost. Fortunately I had secured a photograph of it previously." Not until 1990 did news break that the descendents of Mary Evans had inherited the Springs block, and indeed the whole set of seven blocks, and had sold it that spring to the Maryland Historical Society in Baltimore.

Writing about the quilt dated 1850 and made for Dr. John P. MacKenzie in that ornate, Victorian style which we now identify with Baltimore, Dr. Dunton conjectured, "It is unfortunate that the maker of such a masterpiece of needlecraft should be unknown. . . . Evidently the woman was an artist as is shown by her sense of form and color and probably in a later period would have been a painter. I have a theory which cannot be proved but which seems plausible to me, and that is, that she made her living by making quilts." Manifesting that he was still looking for that "artist," despite having been brought "the work of Mary Evans" some eight years earlier, he immediately follows the 1946 presentation of his theory with an open invitation for help: "It is hoped that old letters or other records will give information as to the name and personality of this wonderful needlewoman."[14] Further on he continued, "I am of the opinion that these designs were probably sold at shops or that they were the work of one woman who practiced quiltmaking as a profession."[15]

In 1974, almost thirty years after the publication of *Old Quilts*, the Orlofskys wrote that "enterprising seamstresses may have supplied quilt block patterns much as needlepoint experts today. It is also believed that a professional needlewoman living in Baltimore, Mary Evans Ford, may have produced a number of these beautiful Baltimore Album quilts, and as many as twenty-six."[16]

Seven years later in the Baltimore Museum of Art's catalog to the 1980–1982 traveling exhibition, Baltimore Album Quilts, Dena Katzenberg again presented the theory of Mary Evans's role in the Baltimore Album Quilts.

An unfinished quilt block, one of a set of seven with pencil lines, and basted appliqués, was brought to the attention of the quilt expert, Dr. William Dunton, by Arthur Evans Bramble. Bramble informed Dr. Dunton that the blocks were the work of his great-aunt, Mary Evans. . . . This piece established some of the hallmarks of Mary Evans's works: triple bowknots, prominent white roses, figures with inked features, the use of rainbow fabrics to indicate contour, a sure sense of formal design, and compositional skill. Such careful elegant work on so many quilts leads to the conclusion that a professional quiltmaker was at work. The author has identified over a dozen quilts which she considers to be the sole work of Mary Evans, and numerous individual blocks on other quilts.[17]

Katzenberg herself, later in her book, is somewhat more tentative about Mary Evans's possible authorship: "There is some reason to believe that the artist of the most proficient work on the Baltimore Album quilts can be identified as Mary Evans."[18] Ms. Katzenberg's research has unearthed a rich trove of information pertinent to these quilts, but on the attribution to Mary Evans it seems not to be conclusive.

In 1987, Schnuppe Von Gwinner's book, *The History of the Patchwork Quilt*, was published. In the chapter on "Friendship and Album Quilts," it states, "Mary Evans and Achsa [sic]

JOANN S. HUDGINS

Godwin [sic] Wilkins of Baltimore were so talented and famous that they sewed whole album quilts and also individual blocks for others commercially."[19] This statement is not footnoted. Dunton is not listed in the bibliography but Katzenberg's *Baltimore Album Quilts* is included. *Baltimore Album Quilts* cites Dunton's *Old Quilts* for four out of six of Katzenberg's notes on Achsah Goodwin Wilkins (1775–1854), including the quote referring to her quiltmaking activity. Katzenberg clearly couches the connection of Wilkins to the Baltimore Album Quilts as her own "hypothesis."[20] Referring back to Dunton as the original source, we find there a quoted reference about Achsah Wilkins by one of her daughters, Mrs. Allen Bowie Davis.[21] But we also find Dunton's forthright statement, "There is no real proof that she [Wilkins] was the maker [of the series of chintz medallion quilts]. . . . It would be pleasant if family tradition held more about the personality of this lady and her habits, especially those connected with her quilt industry, and how she acquired such beautiful chintz patterns for her materials. Perhaps some day one of the old trunks, now in attics, will be cleared and a diary or letters will be found which will give us this information."[22]

Also in 1987, the book *Hearts and Hands* included a statement of Mary Evans's role in these quilts: "We now know from the meticulous research of Dena Katzenberg that many Baltimore album quilts were made with some or all of the blocks designed by professional quiltmaker Mary Evans. . . .The entrance of a professional like Baltimore resident Mary Evans into quiltmaking was a new departure. . . . Mary Evans's procedure [was] . . . supplying prefabricated blocks for which she received payment (and also . . . signing those

"The BAQ journey's possibilities—its rich patterns and beautiful and varied sets—are endless!"
—Karen Moraal

blocks in a standardized script with their donors' names)."[23]

By 1987, had new evidence turned up to confirm these conclusions? The footnote to the above quotation refers the reader back to the pages in Baltimore Album Quilts from which we have already quoted.[24]

Yet it is these subtle shifts of theory into fact that may have set the tone for the confident attribution in January 1989 of Baltimore-style Album Quilts to Mary Evans. An evolution from hypothesis to postulate in the marketplace, parallel to that in the scholarship, is manifested by the repetition of the same set of three paragraphs describing Mary Evans's work being repeated in three consecutive Sotheby catalogs for three different Album Quilts. Sotheby's credits Julie Silber, co-author of *Hearts and Hands*, for those paragraphs. Those excerpts reflect that book's confident view of Mary Evans's role in the authorship of Baltimore Album Quilts. (The actual attributions for these three quilts and their publication sequence are as follows: sale #5680, lot #1463 (January 1988) "Probably Mary Evans"; sale #5755, lot #143 (October 1988) no specific attribution is given in the notation "Variously Signed," but the bulk of this quilt's description consists of discussion of Mary Evans; and, finally, for sale #5810, lot #1106 (January 1989) the stated authorship is "attributed to Mary Evans.")

Attribution to Mary Evans became markedly less ambiguous in the early winter of 1989, following a slower quilt market in the fall of 1988. "Quiet Time for Quilts, Caused by Discriminating Buyers Who Will Settle Only for the Best," pronounced the title of an article by Frank Donegan in *Americana Magazine*. He quoted Nancy Druckman, Sotheby's folkart

GENA HOLLAND

specialist as saying, "We're finding out that these [Baltimore Album Quilts] may not be as rare as we thought. A couple of $100,000 prices show you just how un-rare something is."[25] Perhaps the irony of the story is that to this day the record high-selling quilt, a Baltimore Album Quilt (quilt #2 in Volume 1) and sold by Sotheby's in January 1987, was not attributed to Mary Evans. Her name was not even mentioned in the catalog description although, by January 1989 standards, much of that quilt could have been attributed to her hand. The majority of its blocks are in the ornate, highly realistic, Victorian style associated with her name.

The increasing confidence of Mary Evans attributions for two of the three quilts offered for sale on January 21, 1989, has left a paper trail. From the 1988 publication of Dutton's Quilt Engagement Calendar 1989 to January 1989, the wording changed on the attribution of the Gorsuch Baltimore Album Quilt: "Many blocks . . . may confidently be attributed to the hand of Mary Evans"[26] became "Baltimore Album Quilt, made by the master American Quiltmaker, Mary Evans, circa 1845, for Eleanor [sic] Gorsuch, Baltimore County, Maryland."[27]

Similarly with the Updegraf Album Quilt offered by Christie's, the attribution to Mary Evans had also metamorphosed, though a bit more slowly. In the *Quilt Engagement Calendar 1984*, a description credited to Thomas K. Woodard concerning the Updegraf quilt reads, "It is quite probable that the quilt is the work of Mary Evans." Some five years later, in the New York Times, Rita Reif wrote, "An 1850 Baltimore Album Quilt by Mary Evans, the master quilt maker who created pieced coverlets with patriotic and nostalgic references between 1840 and 1860 is to be auctioned at Christie's."[28] Her article continues, "'She was the first professional quilt maker,' said Jan Wurtzburger, a Christie's folk-art specialist. 'This quilt has all the special hallmarks of her style—the triple bow knot, reticulated baskets, white appliquéd roses, intricate stitching and a careful and deliberate selection of the squares.'" Note the reference to Mary Evans's intricate stitching and reticulated baskets, though neither appear in the City Springs block.

Based on my own experience in examining needlework closely, I'd say the three quilts attributed to Mary Evans and offered for sale in New York that January Saturday contained work by at least three different women. What is the same in all three quilts is the dominant pattern style: ornate, quite realistic, decorative, Victorian. But one style does not mean just one maker. What of the evidence from quilts done in the classic Baltimore Album style today? Some are as breathtaking in the mimicked fabric use and refined needlework as the vintage quilts they replicate. What, beyond age and period fabric, would distinguish these similarly-styled quilts from the originals? Would we always be able to assess whether one person or more than one made a quilt of a uniform style? Again, the present aids our understanding of the past. In the March 1989 issue of *Country Living Magazine*, Mary Roby reviewed the replica[29] of the Metropolitan's Baltimore Album Quilt, circa 1849, attributed in Katzenberg's *Baltimore Album Quilts* to Mary Evans. "It took a year for 30 quilters to complete . . . the quilt's top; . . . [more than] six women completed the quilting in five months." And what was the quality of the work having been done by so many people? "Meticulous uniform quality," the article concludes.

Are there criteria which could help us understand more about who was working in the uniquely Victorian Baltimorean style? I believe so, but even such quantifiable factors as type and length of stitch will not identify a particular quiltmaker beyond all doubt. It's a bit like identifying handwriting done in an archaic calligraphic script on fabric. Hundreds of specimens may be separable into a few gross and inconclusive categories. But studying objective criteria may suggest an answer to the question of one or multiple sewers, for example, of blocks in which fabric and design are similar. And if sufficient data is gathered, a confluence of characteristics may point to a given hand.

Katzenberg concludes, "Such careful elegant work on so many quilts leads to the conclusion that a professional quiltmaker was at work." Yet it is just that "conclusion" that has raised questions among scholars and quiltmakers. That Mary Evans made so many Album Quilts from start to finish just isn't consistent with what contemporary quiltmakers are learning about them. Many of us are making quilts in the classic Baltimore Album style, reproducing classic patterns or designing our own in this style, and keeping track of the hours we spend. I recorded about 50 sewing hours for an ornate Victorian style block like "Silhouette Wreath,"[30] and a bit less for the simpler "Ruched Rose Lyre." Professional quiltmaker Donna Collins, the speediest

appliqué artist I know, reproduced the classic Baltimore Album Quilt block portrait of a manor house in about 40 sewing hours, while Cathy Berry reported up to 60 hours to appliqué an intricate block such as "Red Woven Basket of Flowers."[31]

One professional quiltmaker, Sylvia Pickell, kept a meticulous log of her time making "Immigrant Influences: Album of Heritage."[32] She spent 896 hours on handwork plus 200 hours on design, research, and drawing. Thus 1,096 hours went into making a quilt 72″ square, a bit less than half the square footage of the Baltimore Museum of Art's classic Baltimore Bride Quilt (104″ square) inscribed "To Miss Elizabeth Sliver" and attributed in the Baltimore Museum catalog to Mary Evans. Sylvia Pickell's reckoning indicates a professional seamstress would need at least a year of 40-hour weeks to make one classic Baltimore Album Quilt about 104″ square. Yet the equivalent of well over a dozen quilts have been popularly attributed to one woman, Mary Evans, in roughly a six-year period (1846–1852).

Not only is there an impossible number of quilts attributed to Mary Evans, but additionally, we have only the design style and a method of block preparation to connect to her name. We have no idea how Mary Evans appliquéd: the type, tension, or fineness of her stitch, the color of her thread, or the width and smoothness of her seam. Even when we see identifiable design characteristics, such as the same fabric, or the same skillful draftsmanship, does it prove that one woman made a given block or quilt? I believe not. For one thing, there are significant needlework style differences among blocks attributed to Mary Evans.[33]

To set forth the pivotal differences in style and needlework among the three "Mary Evans" quilts offered for sale January 1989 would require an entire chapter. In short, the quilting of the Sotheby quilt has fewer stitches per inch than the Gorsuch quilt, and both quilts have at least one discolored block suggesting a different foundation fabric or a different age than the surrounding blocks. All three quilts have certain motifs In common. Cornucopias, for example, are found in each, but the blocks differ significantly from quilt to quilt in those elements of style that might separate one maker from another. These elements include fabric use and ink embellishments, how much of the block is filled

JANET GUNN SEWELL

"My love of Baltimore albums has caused me to meet and become really good friends with women from far and near—women that I would never have met otherwise. This connection with other women— women of the past, present, and future— to me is Baltimore's greatest gift."
—Gena Holland

GENE MAY

and in what shape, how compact the bouquets are, and how much white space shows. How are we to know if Mary Evans made some or all of the blocks in any one of these three quilts? What might prove it? Here too, we have the example of contemporary quiltmakers. The current work in classic Baltimore Album style pictured in *Baltimore Beauties and Beyond, Volume 1*,[34] shows just how successfully we can both copy and do original designing in this style almost a century and a half later. If quiltmaking today can so successfully imitate vintage Baltimore, then surely copying, changing, and working "in the style of" may have been going on in mid-nineteenth-century Maryland as well.

Attribution to Mary Evans on the popular level has been incautious. Carefully couched opinions and old theories have given way to confident and detailed assertions. The important point is that if quilts aspire to art, then we need also to strive for the standards of authentication required in fine arts. Increasingly, cautious scholars, for example, are careful not to call a quilt a Baltimore Album Quilt unless "Baltimore" is inscribed on it or unless its provenance from that city or county is documentable. If these proofs are lacking in a quilt that seems in all other respects to fill the bill, they call it a "Baltimore-style Album Quilt." We need this kind of responsible standard in both scholarship and in the marketplace. At least four equally ornate and complex Baltimore Album Quilts are supposed to have been made by Evans in the period from 1849–1850: the Metropolitan's Baltimore Album Quilt, recorded in Katzenberg's Baltimore Album Quilts as circa 1849 (Photo 26 in Volume 1); the Baltimore Museum of Art's Album Quilt inscribed "To Miss Elizabeth Sliver" and "Baltimore, 1849"; the Baltimore Album Quilt inscribed to Dr. John P. Mackenzie and dated "February, 1850";[35] and Christie's Updegraf family quilt, dated 1850. The first three attributions are by Dena Katzenberg, the last, by Christie's. Could Mary Evans, or any one person have made these four quilts in so little time?

The most eloquent, though inconclusive, effort to fix Mary Evans's authorship to specific quilts is Katzenberg's Baltimore Album Quilts. The most potentially concrete evidence proposed is that "One signature of a Mary Evans Ford has been discovered on a 1909 application for admittance to the Aged Women's Home. Analysis of that handwriting suggests that it could have belonged to the person credited with almost half of the finest inscriptions on the quilts."[36] I conferred with the personnel in the Documents Laboratory of the Federal Bureau of Investigation[37] to find out if it was possible to ascertain if the signatures, written some sixty years apart, could have been done by the same hand. "Who knows?" one handwriting expert summed up. "You're never going to get a positive identification. I don't know anyone who would even give a leaning under these circumstances."[38]

To sum up, the "dog that didn't bark" convinced me that the Mary Evans attribution in its present form was questionable. Dunton, of all people, was closest to Evans Bramble's attribution of the basted City Springs block to his Great-Aunt Mary. Whatever conversation passed between Dr. Dunton and Mr. Bramble, Dunton found that set of blocks "entertaining" but seemingly nothing more. The fact that the "dog didn't bark" when it should have for Dr. Dunton, served for me, as in Arthur Conan Doyle's detective story, as pivotal evidence.

The fact may remain, however, that theories about who made these quilts "cannot be proven," as Dr. Dunton wrote almost a half-century ago. New research efforts, inspired by the reappearance of the City Springs Block and already spearheaded by the Maryland Historical Society, will surely turn up exciting new evidence about who made these quilts and why. But no matter who made the classic Baltimore Album Quilts, they are nonetheless national treasures. These heirlooms bind us to our past, give us continuity in the present, and offer us hope for the future. We may not ever be able to affix specific names with certainty to these quilts' design and manufacture. We can learn more about them, though, and in the process learn more about our culture and our past. By so doing we can help attain for these quilts, the work of so many earnest hands, their due regard.

(Endnotes)

1 Material in this chapter was presented by the author as a paper titled. "The Marketing of Mary Evans" at the American Quilt Study Group annual meeting in Bethesda, Maryland, in October 1989. An extract from that paper was subsequently published in the January 1990 issue of *The Magazine Antiques*, pp. 156, 178, and 206.

2 Dunton's correspondence in the Notebooks includes letters from Florence Peto, who also went into print (*Historic Quilts*, New York, American Historical Co., 1939, p. 103) the year after Dunton recorded the 1938 Springs block/Mary Evans, information. Peto echoed Dunton's quest for the professional—but with no mention of Mary Evans. "A feeling persists that many quilts of the Baltimore Bride's type were not made by those whose names were borne on the blocks . . ."

3 Rita Reif, "Auctions," *New York Times*, January 13, 1989.

4 Pat Ferrero, Elaine Hedges, and Julie Silber, *Hearts and Hands: The Influence of Women & Quilts on American Society*, San Francisco, Quilt Digest Press, 1987, p. 36.

5 "The Market," *Arts and Antiques Magazine*, January 1989, p. 46.

6 *Sothby's Catalog*, Sale #5680, Lot #1463 (quilt #9 in the Color Section).

7 *National Antiques Review*, February 1972, p. 21.

8 Three major antiques sales were held the same January 1989 weekend at Christie's Auction House, Sotheby's Auction House, and the annual New York Winter Antiques Show at the New York Armory.

9 *Sotheby's Catalog*, Sale #5810, Lot#l106.

10 Patsy and Myron Orlofsky, *Quilts in America*.

11 Marilyn Bordes, *Twelve Great Quilts from the American Wing*, New York, Metropolitan Museum of Art, 1974.

12 Dunton, *Notebooks*, Album VIII, pp.128–35. The text of the seven-page manuscript, dated 1938, reads in part:

KATHLEEN L. OSGOOD

Back around 1850 there seems to have been a fashion of making quilts of an unusual character for presentation to some favored man or woman, often a clergyman. It was natural for the ladies of the congregation to show their regard by making a quilt to commemorate his incumbency.

Among the quilts which I have met which are associated with churches or are of this presentation type perhaps the most entertaining is not a quilt but merely the makings as the various blocks have not been joined. One of these was made by Mary Evans Ford (1830–1928) when she was twenty years old, or in 1850, a member of the Caroline Street Methodist Church, not far from City Springs Square, Pratt and Eden Streets, Baltimore, Maryland . . .

Miss Ford evidently had an attachment to the neighborhood for what was evidently intended to be the large central block of the quilt has in its centre a view of the park with the pavilion which covered the spring or "fountain," done in shaded browns which gives a high light effect to the supporting pillars and also to the trunks of the trees which flank it. . . . The maker was an artist with a wonderful flair for color harmony and of the value of light and shadow so that her perspective is exceptionally well handled. The piece is unfinished as all pieces to be appliquéd are basted on the white ground but the effect is quite beautiful. The muslin is 72 threads to the inch.

Accompanying this which was to have been the centre of an album quilt were six eighteen-inch blocks some of which are signed. . . . The most striking is that depicting the minister which is unsigned. . . . His head and face are partly inked and partly painted. The collar of his coat is broad and is appliquéd separately. His right arm extends down and the painted hand is holding a red edged open book marked "Hymns." His left hand (painted) rests on a tan and yellow book marked "Bible" which is on a red table. Above his head is an inked eagle with a scroll on which is "John W. Hall." (Quoted by permission of Baltimore Museum of Art.)

Dunton then goes on to describe the remaining blocks in the set One with "quite a conglomeration of symbols" (some that he describes are shared by both Odd Fellows and Masons) and the mime, "Nathaniel Lee" inscribed thereon; a "horn" (cornucopia) of "rather ungraceful" flowers and leaves, a heart of "angular leaves" outlined inside and out with a row of quarter-inch berries, and a cutwork square with a "a coarse red rose" on each side and parallel strips of small hexagons intertwined by rosevine. He concludes with subsequent history concerning the City Springs Square and its neighborhood in Baltimore.

13 Dunton himself long investigated questions raised by the set of seven blocks, as he did so many subjects touched upon by these quilts. His 1938 description of the seven blocks reflects research into the demographics of the City Springs area and the evolution of the Baltimore water system. Two years later, a 1940 letter (in the Notebook files) shows that Dunton was still researching the identity of John W. Hall whose name and whose portrait, apparently, appear in one these seven blocks. Page 7 of this Album VIII article gives us yet another due about John Hall: "It is known that he assisted at laying the cornerstone of Grace Church." This may be a clue to understanding this block, for early histories of Baltimore repeatedly note the laying of various cornerstones in the first half of the nineteenth century as "presided over by the Masons" and as attended by "Masonic ritual."

14 Dunton, *Old Quilts*, p. 41.

15 *Ibid.*, p. 118.

16 Orlofsky, *Quilts in America*, p. 239.

17 Dena Katzenberg, *Baltimore Album Quilts*, pp. 61–62.

18 *Ibid.*, p. 98.

19 Schnuppe Von Gwinner, *The History of the Patchwork Quilt, Origins, Traditions and Symbols of a Textile Art*, Munich, Keyser Book Publishing, 1987, p. 138.

20 Katzenberg, *Baltimore Album Quilts*, pp. 64–65.

FRAN LOPES

21 Dunton, *Old Quilts*, pp. 202–203.

22 *Ibid.*, pp. 195–199.

23 Ferrero, Hedges, and Silber, *Hearts and Hands*, pp. 34–36.

24 Katzenberg, *Baltimore Album Quilts*, pp. 61–62.

25 Frank Donegan, "In the Marketplace: Quiet Time for Quilts," *Americana Magazine*, Fall, 1988, p. 64.

26 *Quilt Engagement Calendar 1989*; this quilt illustrated May 7–13.

27 America Hurrah Antiques advertisement, Winter Antiques Show Catalog. January 1989, p. 45, in *The Magazine Antiques*, January 1989, unnumbered advertising page; and in *The Clarion*, Winter 1989, p. 7.

28 Reif, "Auctions," *New York Times*, January 3,1989.

29 This replica was made by the East Bay Heritage Quilters. The estimated hours to quilt this were provided by Adele Ingraham and Janet Shore, leaders of the project.

30 Sienkiewicz, *Baltimore Beauties and Beyond, Volume I*, Color Plate 24.

31 *Ibid.*, Color Plate 35.

32 *Ibid.*, Photo 31.

33 *Ibid.*, pp. 102–103.

34 *Ibid.*, pp. 81–96 and 107.

35 Dunton, *Old Quilts*, pp. 31–43; and Roxa Wright, "Baltimore Friendship Quilt," *Woman's Day Magazine*, Fall 1965, pp. 52, 53, and 90.

36 Katzenberg, *Baltimore Album Quills*, p. 62. Further discussion of signatures is found on pp. 68–69.

37 Bill Carter of the Federal Bureau of Investigation Press Department, co-ordinator, with FBI Documents Laboratory personnel, interview by the author, Washington, D.C., February 28, 1989.

38 Another expert added, "Even your own handwriting changes over the years. Injury, illness, even the intention to change your own handwriting affects it. When we do handwriting comparisons we don't like to deal with writing that is over five years apart [from the identified specimen]. You cannot associate writing without same-time writing samples."

"Could you ever say positively that one person could have written many different names on these quilts?" I asked. The response was, "Absolutely not. There might be some letter combinations in common that might suggest a possibility, however remote. But the phrases being compared [or the names being signed] have to be the same for purposes of positively identifying authorship." Katzenberg offers both diverse names and varied inscriptions for comparison to Mary Evans Ford's signature (pp. 62 and 68 in *Baltimore Album Quilts*). Furthermore, it was noted in the interview that the samples would have to be "natural and free-flowing and on the same surface," not a comparison between one done on paper and others done on fabric. "Writing with ink on fabric is by definition contrived, not natural and free-flowing."

Observing that greater uniformity of penmanship and closer conformity to a calligraphic ideal were characteristic of the mid-nineteenth century, one expert said, "They were stricter then. The longer a person stayed with an intent to write in the Copperplate Hand, the chances are even less that an association could be made." She noted that she could not connect my signature on a free-flowing letter with my careful signature on a quilt block.

Myth, Dreams, Metaphors and Magic:
Album Quilts at Exhibition

Elly Sienkiewicz gave these introductory remarks at the Press Preview Party just prior to the opening of C&T Publishing's Baltimore Album Revival Exhibition and Contest, held at the Lancaster Host Hotel, Lancaster, Pennsylvania, on April 7–10, 1994.

GOOD EVENING AND WELCOME! Thank you all so much for coming to our party, for coming to our exhibition. It's a particular pleasure to address you at this festive tribute to Revivalist Baltimore Album Quilts. Thank you, too, to Rita Barber, whose Quilters' Heritage Celebration provides the forum for our show. And thank you to our Contest Judges, Editors Bonnie Leman of *Quilter's Newsletter Magazine*, and Mary Roby of *Country Living*. Thank you to our hosts here, my publisher, C&T Publishing, represented tonight by its President, Todd Hensley. As you may know, I have had the great good fortune to have C&T as my publisher for the *Baltimore Beauties and Beyond* series. Their commitment to publish the series has abided as my interest in these quilts has deepened. My second book on these classic quilts, *Baltimore Beauties and Beyond, Studies in Classic Album Quilt Appliqué, Volume I*, has, since the series was begun in 1989, mushroomed (nourished by these old quilts' unfolding secrets) into seven books so far.

A bit to my amazement, as I became captivated by the antebellum Baltimores, so did growing numbers of quiltmakers both across the country and around the world. Considering the question "What is this fascination with the Baltimore Album style?" seems an appropriate introduction to viewing this much anticipated quilt show. We must ask, too, why so many international citizens currently find creation in the appliquéd Album format not only intriguing, but downright compelling. What meaning, what pleasure, what impetus to self-expression, what search for solace has brought these quilts to life? What magic of heart and mind and hand has appliquéd such beauty into these Album Quilts?

Perhaps these are unanswerable questions! But let's consider them just briefly, as a background melody for viewing these stitched and showcased glories. "Only through Art," wrote Marcel Proust, "can we emerge from ourselves and know what another sees." To begin our visit, then, let's slip back a century and more, and breathe, for a moment, the ether of earlier times. A gentleman named Edward Everett, in an address at Buffalo, New York, on October 9, 1857, phrased an appealing thought: "As a work of art," he began, "I know few things more pleasing to the eye, or more capable of affording scope and gratification to a taste for the beautiful, than a well-situated, well-cultivated farm." Wedding both art and craft, that quote seems wonderfully applicable here in Lancaster, surrounded by Pennsylvania's rolling farmfield patchwork.

May I speak for us all and say that we ourselves know few things more pleasing to the eye, or more gratifying to a taste for the beautiful, than a well laid-out, well-stitched quilt? For as surely as the plowman follows his calling to sow and to reap, tilling the land for food, quiltmakers heed their craft's pull to art. These quilts we make are sustaining fruit, capable of nourishing souls as surely as farmers' wheat nourishes bodies.

Vintage political philosophy, too, smiles on our likening a quilt's pleasing quality to that of a well laid-out farm. Some two centuries ago, Thomas Jefferson favored an agrarian economy for his young country, arguing that land ownership gave citizens a sense of freedom and independence. Moreover, he believed that the occupation of farming, a way of life tied close to nature, would nurture man's innately good human character, his moral nature, and his common sense. By the same logic, could we not argue, that Album Quilt-making gives one a sense of freedom and independence, ties one close to nature, and is good for democracy? [(Aside) You can rest easy now; that's as close as I come to discussing politics!] Both farming and Album Quilt-making are complex undertakings requiring a dream—a vision of the whole—

MYTH *must be kept alive. The people who can keep it alive are artists of one kind of another. The function of the artist is the mythologization of the environment and the world. . . . But he has to be an artist who understands mythology and humanity and isn't simply a sociologist with a program for you. The . . . ideas and poetry of the traditional cultures come out . . . of an elite experience of people particularly gifted, whose ears are open to the song of the universe. These people speak to the folk, and there is an answer from the folk. . . . But the first impulse in the shaping of a folk tradition comes from above, not from below.*

—Joseph Campbell
with Bill Moyers,
The Power of Myth

AUTHOR'S NOTE:
Wow! Like quiltmakers. . .

GENA HOLLAND

AUTHOR'S NOTE:
Are Album Quilts for us a mythology? Does their imagery, their making, help us make sense out of life? Our ritual repetition of symbolic designs does have the tenor of rite. Appliqué's monotonous Tack Stitch does have a peaceful rhythm, a meditative quality. . . Quiltmaking is a comfort; does staunch a hunger. . .

and a square-by-square approach to accomplishing the task.

Jefferson suggests that as the farmer cultivates the soil, something is cultivated within the farmer, himself: something transforming, something "magical" happens to him. Does quiltmaking similarly transform the quiltmaker? Ask almost any Album Quilt-maker and she will say that it is so. We've long proceeded on the assumption that the whole is equal to the sum of its parts. Yet we know that in certain endeavors—in art or in sports for example—the whole can be much more. Five boys playing basketball don't necessarily constitute a Team with a capital "T." A Team is much more than the sum of its parts. It creates something magical.

A great quilt, too, is more than the sum of its parts. As we wait for the quilt show doors to open, we must all be curious about what we'll see. When we contemplate these quilts, each of us will most likely be weaving a braid, a 'cord of judgment' composed of some version of these three questions: 1. "What do these works of art, these Revivalist Baltimore Album Quilts actually look like?" 2. "While the artist was making this work of art, was she affected by the process? Did something magical happen to her?" And 3. "When we, the audience, see these quilts how do they affect us? Will some of that magic be conveyed to us?" For we can hypothesize that to the degree to which a quilt affects its viewer, to that degree the quilt is more art than craft.

Tonight, an evening in nature's most optimistic season, we're here to celebrate Baltimore-style Album Quilts. We come in tribute both to modern masterpieces and to heirlooms made a century and a half ago. The year 1994 draws us close to the cusp of our own century's turn. And thus the time, the place, and the occasion seem auspicious. In choosing both an exhibition and a competition as the arena for our festivities, C&T Publishing echoes a mid-19th Century host, The Maryland Institute for the Promotion of the Mechanic Arts. The Institute displayed

Baltimore's Album Quilts at a series of major annual exhibitions. Beginning with the first exhibit in 1848, they, too, produced a catalog of "articles deposited at the exhibition," and included, thereafter, the annual opening and closing addresses. Baltimore Albums thus thread our century to its predecessor, and they will, we have to believe, piece these centuries, past and present, to those yet to come.

To identify the quilts we fête tonight, Cleda Jeannette Dawson, curator of 1992's Great Baltimore Revival show in Jefferson, Oregon, coined the term "Revivalist Baltimore Albums." This name seems to suit them best. It does honor to their antebellum roots while recognizing the inventiveness of a style come freshly into its own. As all Albums (whether record albums, stamp albums, autograph or photograph albums) are collections on a theme, so Album Quilts are collections of blocks, most appliquéd, on a theme. Today's Albums include both faithfully reproduced traditional motifs, many used intentionally for their symbolic meanings, and original designs with meanings of their own.

In popular usage, the term "Baltimore Album Quilts" has become a rather loose one, an evolution that may already have begun in the era of their making. By name and by geography, classic Baltimore Album Quilts of the 1840s through the mid-1850s, have always been tied most directly to Baltimore City, Maryland. But even in the mid-19th Century, we perceive the style as dynamic and contagious. In varying degrees, elements of the style extended beyond Baltimore and metamorphosed, reflecting grand historic change as well as the individual stitchers' particular history. It blended with Album styles well north, south, and west of the city that lent it its name.

The incorporation of appliquéd symbols—those visible signs of invisible things—is fundamental to the Baltimore Album style. Inclusion of the symbolic tongue, in fact, characterizes the whole of Victorian literary, musical, and material culture. But it is the fraternal symbols, in particular—those of the Masons, and especially those of America's Baltimore-centered Odd Fellows[1]—which blaze such a visible and far-reaching trail of Albums. If one followed only the Odd Fellow's Three-Linked Chain symbol (for "Friendship, Love, and Truth,") its stylistic trail winds well beyond Maryland. The appliqués seem both to have been inspired by, and to decorate Independent Odd Fellowdom's meteoric rise in popularity in this country.

Let me, at this point, sketch just the briefest reference frame, so that both those who already know and love Baltimore-style Albums well, and those first meeting the style this evening, will share some common footing. This show's catalog will not be my last book on the Baltimore-style Albums, which is simply to say that my love for them has been both ardent and enduring. I won't even attempt to note here what those books try to impart about the classic Baltimore Album Quilts. This is not the time to focus on their brilliant Victorian needlework threads; nor is it the place to examine their bright snatches of political and cultural history; nor will I try, tonight, to do much more than recall for you the warp of momentous social change (so similar to our own society today) upon which this rich Album tapestry was woven. We can only mention the massive waves of immigration, and the disintegration of the family-centered economy as industrialization and urbanization changed the very texture of those quiltmakers' cloth.

The need for fellowship, for common values, and for a sense of belonging was increasingly served, not as it had been, by extended families, but by expanding institutions: churches, fraternal orders, friendly benefit societies, and educational institutions like the Maryland Institute for the Promotion of the Mechanic Arts. I personally believe Baltimore's antebellum quiltmakers stitched their old world's symbols together with emblems of the new; I believe that by their quiltmaking they navigated the shoals of societal change and transited safely to firm ground. I might wonder aloud, tonight, whether we are presently witnessing Album Quilt-making's healing ritual repeated once again. Let me share just a few hypotheses with you about why quiltmakers today seem to be so taken by this antebellum style. For you will see that they are learning this classic style's intricacies well, and some already have gone on to something quite "beyond Baltimore," quite distinctly and evocatively their own.

I first met a number of the "classic Baltimores," these fascinating ladies, in person at the Baltimore Museum of Art's 1982 exhibition. Immediately and forcefully, their bright beauty drew me to them. Irresistibly, a sense that they were windows to the souls of the women who made them, intrigued me. And an intuition that they spoke in a forgotten symbolic tongue led, in 1983, to *Spoken Without a Word,* my first book on the genre. Through faithfully reproduced Album block patterns, it strives to convey that style's artistry.

Though just 11 years ago, by a certain measure *Spoken Without a Word* was written in a quite different era. Today Victorian eclecticism surrounds us: It is revived in clothing, in architecture, in decorative arts, and in interior décor. Victoriana once again abounds in magazines, gift volumes, and all manner of paper ephemera. With it has come, inevitably, more familiarity with that era's sensibilities, its loyal fellowships, and its overt spirituality. In 1983, no miniature reprints of the Language of Flowers decorated bookstore shelves as they do now, and few of us even remembered this symbolic tongue's existence. Thus when in that first book, I suggested that the Baltimore Album Quilts used an iconogra-

METAMORPHOSIS, or symbol-formation; the origin of human culture. A laurel branch in the hand, a laurel wreath on the house, a laurel crown on the head; to purify and celebrate. Apollo after slaying the old dragon, or Roman legions entering the city in triumph. Like in the Feast of Tabernacles; or Palm Sunday. The decoration, the mere display is poetry: making this thing other. A double nature.

—Norman O. Brown, "Daphne, or Metamorphosis" (Joseph Campbell, Editor, *Myths, Dreams, and Religion*)

AUTHOR'S NOTE: *Beautiful! All the laurel wreaths, then and now—in Album quilts!*

JESSICA LAMAR

IN *a Navajo hogan
... the fireplace is
in the center, which
becomes a cosmic
center, with the smoke
coming up through
the hole in the ceiling
so that the scent of
the incense goes to
the nostrils of the
gods. The landscape,
the dwelling place,
becomes an icon,
a holy picture.
Wherever you are,
you are related to the
cosmic order.*

—Joseph Campbell
with Bill Moyers,
The Power of Myth

AUTHOR'S NOTE:
*Just like the fraternal
imagery in the classic
Albums: all those "urns
of incense representing
the sweet soul ascending
heavenward." And the
Rebekahs, stitching
symbolic flowers rising
from neo-classic glassware.
All those icons in appliqué:
all those baskets of
blessings, those grateful
cornucopias filled to
overflowing with the earth's
bounty . . . and Liberty's.*

phy, a symbolic language, I was most tentative. I simply included a lexicon of symbols and the suggestion that these often-ancient symbols spoke intentionally of specific lives and times.

Tested now, for more than a decade, the theory that these quilts spoke without words seems proven true. Moreover, we've deciphered key emblems of whole "world views" through quilt-borne symbols of Baltimore's fraternal orders. Then, too, we've sensed history's pageantry in these quilts through military insignia and memorials, through flag-borne stars marking the entry of new states into the Union, and through the logos of such social movements as Temperance and Abolition. Thus, to one who listens, the symbols in the antique Albums can carry you well beyond the individual's experience, and when they reflect what is most deeply felt they reach that which is universal.

Makers of the classic Albums used old, even ancient, archetypes and symbols. Borrowing them to inform their own experience, they made the old at once both old and new. Generations later, repeating this quiltmaking ritual, contemporary Album Quiltmakers stitch the same symbols one again. Thus the old is reborn into a new system of symbols related to the present and to each quiltmaker's particular history. Some turn-of-the-20th-century quiltmakers seem uniquely attuned to antiquarian symbolism, reporting that they like not only the Baltimore Albums' objective designs, but also the subjective sentiments those quilts convey. Commonly this recognition is phrased modestly, almost shyly: "I like what the quilts say" is how it's most often put, with no elaboration. But once, after a class, a conversation among a couple of Album makers summed up these feelings:

I like the message in the Albums. I like the gentleness with which it is delivered. . . . So much that we hold passionately private, is put publicly in our faces today, whether it be cherished religious beliefs or the intimacy of sexual bonds. It makes precious things ordinary, vulgar.

One thing I love about the Albums is the delicacy of their expression. There is an air of restraint, even in their overabundance.

All contemporary Album makers seem to impute some personal meaning to the patterns they choose to stitch and to the very making of their Albums. Almost uniformly, they report that making their Albums gave them pleasure, that "It was a happy time for me." Several have spoken, though, of overwhelming loss, of the death of a child or of a spouse, of stitching their way through an Album to mend the hole in their life's fabric. "And I began to heal," one summed up simply. "It worked. It pulled me back." Though I have since gone on to write much more about Baltimore's Albums, those two threads—the artistic and the symbolic—which first I picked up in *Spoken Without a Word*, still entwine brightly for me, making Album Quilts the stuff of myth and dreams.

With such enthusiastic endorsements, perhaps we should take a closer look at what might be making Album Quiltmakers so happy. Beyond a doubt, the happiness of making even the simplest Album stems in part from the habitual and joyful affirmation of beauty in everyday life. The Album mode encourages this. With flowers as the Album's common tongue, how could it not be so? Even tragedy recorded in an Album has been integrated with the peace of acceptance and the beauty of understanding. I sometimes picture the Album maker as an olden-day lady taking the air along muddy, malodorous city streets. Rather than succumb to depressive unpleasantness, we're told that the wise mistress would hold fragrant posies called the "tussie-mussies" high, so that their sweet floral scents would obscure the stink around her. Even the simplest Baltimore-style Album, antique or revivalist, is garlanded with nature's fragrant bounty. Like counting one's blessings, choosing blocks for an Album Quilt can only cheer and uplift one. Such Pollyanna-ish optimism may not be politically correct, but the sweet sensation is so pleasurable as to be habit-forming!

Album Quiltmakers seem increasingly to see themselves as a fellowship or even a family. This is not surprising since some now call quiltmaking a "subculture," noting that by the following traits, it qualifies. Quiltmaking has: 1. its own charismatic leaders (teachers, authors, books, magazines, publishers, and conference impresarios); 2. its own annual visits to favorite watering holes (as well as guilds, meetings, and "bees"); 3. its own unique regalia; and 4. its own rites, like challenges and making raffle quilts. Album Quiltmakers, themselves, seem recently to feel united in an identifiable quiltmaker subgroup—one with their own teachers, books, pins, tote bags, block carriers, fabrics, shows, and, now, a contest! When I teach an Album class these days, whether here or abroad, the people who attend seem to have a cohesiveness, a self-confidence; they seem quite certain that though among strangers, they are yet among friends and right where they belong. Some say they feel they know me from my books, and I feel I know something important about them. With increasing frequency, individuals come back repeatedly for more classes, and may promise, "You'll see me again." And surely this sense of belonging, of being as with those-who-travel-together, of sharing values, of having common goals is something we all hunger for in our society's explosive numbers and dizzying rates of change.

Pop-psychology, too, offers, in the term "flow," an explanation for why Album Quiltmakers find the experience so compelling, so fulfilling, and so downright exhilarating. When once I asked a quilt class why the needleart of the Baltimore Albums so enthralled us, the consensus answer was, "It's a recognition of excellence." In fact that recognition actually defines a classic style, "a style that sets a standard for all time." The artistic heights of the old Maryland Albums have been broadly acknowledged by both the quilt world and the art and antique world. Back in 1983, I had held a block contest based on the patterns in *Spoken Without a Word*. I wanted to test whether numbers of 20th-century women could once again create in the fine-scale appliqué of the classic Albums. Frankly, I wasn't sure we could. For, by the mid-1980s, only a handful of modern quiltmakers had made Revivalist Baltimore Albums. Among the earliest to receive public acclaim was Bernice Enyeart of Indiana. Pat Cox of Minnesota designed Albums with elements of that style, and Nancy Pearson of Illinois interpreted appliquéd Albums in delightfully original floral appliqués.

That initial contest's seven winners became the first needleartists for my *Baltimore Beauties* series. By 1984, I myself had begun intensively to appliqué, researching the needleart as well as writing on the history of these quilts. But like the seamless emergence of a bud into full bloom, my "Baltimore" classes, by 1986, were increasingly in demand. *Lady's Circle Patchwork Quilts'* Editor, Carter Houck, had even titled the moment, calling that period one of "Baltimore Album Revival." In 1988, C&T agreed to publish *Baltimore Beauties and Beyond, Volume I,* and by 1989, we had the first national show of Revivalist Baltimore Albums in Archbold, Ohio. Sauder Farm and Craft Village sponsored the show for which I'd obtained just half a dozen or so Albums, three of them group-made. But that small exhibition was packed daily by crowds who lingered long, seemingly enraptured. Once again, a century and a half later, Baltimore's contagion had begun. Watching the watchers, I could almost sense in the air their growing urge to test their skills, to go for this "peak quilting experience."

"Optimal experience," University of Chicago professor, Mihaly Csikszentmihalyi, tells us, occurs when we're engrossed in a mental or physical challenge. In his book, *Flow: The Psychology of Optimal Experience,* he concludes that we're happiest meeting a challenge sufficiently difficult to be stimulating but not so hard that it's beyond our ability to attain.

If we measure the flow theory's checklist against Album Quiltmaking, we learn some-

ANNE CARTER

THE *sanctification of the local landscape is a fundamental function of mythology.*
—Joseph Campbell with Bill Moyers, *The Power of Myth*

AUTHOR'S NOTE:
We also feel a part of the natural world. . .

A WORLD *ends when
its metaphor has died.
It perishes when those
images, though seen,
No longer mean.*

— Archibald
MacLeish,
"Hypocrite Auteur,"
*Collected Poems,
1917–1952*

THE *Indian boy
was saying there is a
shining point where
all lines intersect. . . .
God is an intelligible
sphere—a sphere
known to the mind,
not to the senses—
whose center is
everywhere and whose
circumference is
nowhere.*

—Joseph Campbell
with Bill Moyers,
The Power of Myth

AUTHOR'S NOTE:
*Like the "All-Seeing Eye of
God" icon on so many old
Baltimore Album Quilts.
Like the All-Seeing Eye of
God in my purse—atop
every dollar bill's pyramid!
Is this part of why we love
the Albums so? They bring
back ancient symbols,
help us hear forgotten
metaphors, help us
understand our place in
the universe?*

thing. The theory postulates six elements as crucial for "flow" to happen: 1. The task must test our skills. 2. It must focus our complete attention. 3. It must offer us clear, attainable goals. 4. We must be able to lose both ourselves and, 5. our sense of time while working to meet the challenge. And 6. We must feel totally in command of the present moment. How can these possibly be attained, you might wonder? To create a hand-appliquéd, hand-quilted Album, one has accepted a challenge comparable to a climber taking on Mt. Everest. But the challenge is incremental, the instructions detailed, and the gratification comes in small bites all along the way.

Talk about attainable goals: these Albums where you make one block at a time provide the ultimate in step-by-step feedback. When a quiltmaker begins with *Volume I's* Lesson 1, she sets out to perfect the cut-away appliqué method whose whole short-term goal is to stitch just 2″ or so at a time. (Out of such tiny grains of sand are mighty mountains made.) But, you might well ask, how does a person feel when she's worked at her blocks a year and has just two or four or six of them done? The answer is: Proud. Quietly, gently, but indisputably, proud. For this quiltmaking genre seems to carry its own philosophy: "The happiness is in the journey, not at the end of the road." There is a wonderful "You can do it" attitude as stitchers encourage each other; and a whole paraphernalia of block carriers, from appliquéd cases to printed pizza boxes, has evolved among Album makers for storing and displaying their squares. By 1991, it crossed my mind that these showpiece blocks, these treasured possessions, had begun to take on a life of their own, somewhat like purchased fabric too beautiful to cut into. Along with pride, one could feel a certain contentment of accomplishment settling in: With such a prettily packaged and so much admired Album block collection, who, really, was anxious to finish her quilt? Who wanted to rush and thereby, perhaps end this pleasant journey?

Into this peaceful scene, C&T dropped their 1994 Baltimore Album Revival Con-test. Contests are not everyone's cup of tea. But quilt contests provide miracle-working incentives for some. Thus C&T's contest lit a spark that raised the Album makers' "optimal experience meter" to fever pitch! The aspiration to be Number One, to gain accolades and fame is natural to Man. Historically it has led to great accomplishments. On the other hand, "elitism" is currently disparaged. One hears that among top colleges and universities, the trend is to give everyone a "Gentleman's A" lest professors be forced to make invidious distinctions, or perhaps hurt feelings, or by so doing damage someone's self esteem. But imagine human history without some recognizably best and brightest, or perhaps with no freedom to excel noticeably, or no incentive to strive harder.

Sponsoring a contest invites honorable pride and rewards the desire to stand out. In a quiltmaker, these traits can lead to great quilts. Without a doubt, the Maryland Institute exhibitions of the 1840s and 1850s helped spur the original Baltimore Album Quilts on to classic heights. One can almost watch the evolution take place within those quilts as the quiltmakers learned from one another, learned from one year's quilts to the next, and got better. Plato (as translated by Alan Bloom, in his *The Closing of the American Mind*) called such admirable ambition the "search of spiritedness for legitimate self-expression." Thus, once C&T's contest was announced, exhilaration peaked rapidly, then held solidly for almost a year before the October 1993 deadline. When we enter the exhibit hall, you and I may even be able to assess the oceans of "Flow" enjoyed, simply by estimating the yards of quilting thread used!

To be fair about it, flow or peak experience can be present throughout all of quilt-making. But I like to call Album Quilts the "Outward Bound" of quiltmaking. Few quilt styles are richly faceted enough to engross a quiltmaker so completely as do these, and for so long. And few quilt genres are meaty enough to fuel seven books—and counting—from a single pen. The wealth to be had is not just in the technical challenge; it is also in the inward journey the Album maker takes—unfolding her heart and soul through the meditative work of her hands. As though to mark their depth of meaning for us, quiltmaking's phrases have entered the language as powerful figures of speech. Quiltmaking's metaphors, those images that make dissimilar things into a harmonious, even beautiful, whole, ease the quiltmaker's understanding of her life and times.

The Album maker sifts through that which is meaningful enough to record, that which is transient, that which she can hope to change, that which the quiltmaking will help her to accept. To plain, utilitarian cloth we stitch decorative beauty, where another might not have. The stuff of making Album blocks, this stitching of icons and abundance, unlocks our powers of memory and imagination. We find some continuity, some universals in the old emblems' meanings while some we imbue with secrets of our own. Continuity and contradiction. Our life is like an Album—much of it a given, but many of the steps along the way are taken by choice. We hope our Album will find favor, tie us to each other; speak, for us still, when we no longer stitch and quilt. And if the quiltmaker's love is the antique Albums, she sews with a sense of history that aids her perception of what she's come from, who she is, and where she's going.

It's almost time for the Baltimore Revival Exhibit to open its doors. What you see will, I think, please and impress you. You will see quilts made singly and in groups, by women whom you probably do not yet know. Some of the quilts will sing in a loud clear voice with a song meant for you to hear. Some sing more softly, almost to themselves. Like my first visit with the old ones, you, too, may sense that these quilts are speaking to you without words, in the symbolic mode. But it would take a long visit to hear what some Albums would say when you knew them better. In the exhibition hall, the essay submitted with each quilt has been hung behind the quilt in a plastic sleeve. I hope you'll get the chance

to read a bit of what each quiltmaker shares there, as well.

Their bright colors and full-bloomed beauty drew me to the Baltimores 12 years ago. And their symbolism has held me since, as though it nourished me with something long hungered for. The psychologist Carl Jung wrote that we have suffered "an unprecedented impoverishment of symbols." To have seen the Gulf War's yellow ribbons waving across the land, it seems that this is so. We are a people longing for common ground, seeking a way to unite, and we seem unable to do it through words. Words set us to arguing, magnify our differences. Symbols, because they speak without words, speak directly to our hearts.

It would not overstate the case to say that Baltimore-style Album Quilts obsess me. It is as though, for me, Album Quilts have become the myth, the imagery, by which I make sense out of much of life. Of all curious topics to send me back to the Albums for answers, a recent trip to Manhattan caught me engrossed by territorial turf fighting street gangs, and their symbols. Our nation's capital is my hometown. When I travel to lecture I'm repeatedly asked, "Do you actually live right *in* Washington, D.C.?" And to that question which conveys incredulity, I answer "Yes, right in the city." As you know it is among the world's most beautiful burghs, but as legendary now for its crime as for its culture.

Last spring though, I was as wide-eyed as a country girl when in New York City for the Great American Quilt Festival. As in an echo, I heard myself asking members of the Manhattan Quilt's Guild, "Do you really live right *in* New York City?" Then when my colleague pointed out that the ornate graffiti we passed each day were gang symbols marking territory, I got so excited: Brotherhoods, icons, secrets—stuff of the Album Quilts! One elaborate, quite lovely symbol had been sprayed in metallic gold paint through a cut stencil.

MARY K. TOZER

AUTHOR'S NOTE:
Album makers say, "Commit to one choice at a time. Let the quilt 'talk to you,' saying what comes next."

EDIE ZAKEM

WHATEVER *the reasons that a person embarks on the continuous communication between the inner and outer worlds, whether because of a compulsion or because of a calling, it seems that if he remains committed to the dialectical process, something new and unexpected emerges in his life. It is as though the core of a center forms within him. A new self forms, not from his directly seeking it, but as a side effect of the integrity with which he continues his inner-outer journey.*

—Ira Progoff,
*Waking Dream and
Living Myth*

That motif, like the young men who served us in that district's street markets, looked Middle Eastern. Later, in the mail, the same quiltmaker friend sent me a promised flyer of further gangland information from the U.S. Marshall's Office. The pamphlet explained how a symbol crossed out or drawn on top of, witnessed a territorial takeover. It noted that gangs wore special "colors" or identifiable regalia, and explained that secret handsigns were signals, signs of recognition between "brothers."

And I thought of the myth, and of the Album Quilts, of the fraternal order handsigns, of how even the Boy Scout Handshake must be connected to this need for acknowledging a brother, for identifying with one's own. I thought of how excited the women must have been when, in 1886, the Brotherhood officially recognized a Sisterhood—the Rebekahs.[2] Now *that* coming was something to stitch into life's Album! And I pondered modern quiltmaking, all of us ladies and a few men, as itself a subculture. April a year ago, right there in front of the Museum of American Folk Art on West 62nd Street, two polarities—the quiltmakers and urban gang members—touched. Each informed the other. That moment when they touched floodlit something I'd not seen before. Through antique Baltimore's myth, I understood something about our common humanity: ours and that of our needlesisters of yore; ours and that of the youthful street gangs. Through the Album metaphor, I realized how we all need so to belong. I thought I'd spotted another common thread. [Might I tonight be mischievously uncool? Might I share from this public podium the suspicion that I may be an uninitiated member of the "Album Gang"? This sense of belonging feels good. And hey! Album makers are my kind of people!]

I've confessed to you that these are Album-colored glasses through which I see the world, so it should not surprise you that I found quilts in an essay by Jodi Daynard from

The New York Times Book Review of March 28, 1993. It was titled "Floppy Discs are Only Knowledge, But Manuscripts are Wisdom." Like so much that I read these days, this piece on manuscripts became a metaphor for me about Album Quilts. Ms. Daynard expressed herself so beautifully that I'd like to conclude tonight's address by paraphrasing one of her paragraphs, rewriting it as though it spoke not of manuscripts, but of quilts:

In many ways quilts are the most fragile and humble of human products. More often than not a quilt records but a tiny vicissitude of time, one soul stitching across the mental rapids from one stone to another, in the eternal hope of getting somewhere. And yet, looking at a quilt, one sees a wholeness; one feels—if only momentarily—wise. Perhaps this is because the true beauty of a quilt lies not so much in what it reveals as what it hides. Quilts, like other art, contain a powerful core of mystery. How is it after all, that I can study a vintage Baltimore Album Quilt and, by dint of smell, almost feel the maker's presence as surely as the blind feel a tree before they touch it? Somewhere in this mystery lies the mystery of our connectedness to others. Not literally—in the sense of shared conversations or relatives, nor even of shared theologies, but spiritually, as in a shared understanding: An understanding that cloth shreds, threads break; that the fine stitches of our young and middle years inevitably yield to the stiffened hands of old age. Soon, very soon, quilts seem to tell us, we will be nothing more than the fine-stitched—or simply basted—blocks we leave behind.

But though just threads, these quilts are the thread of a life here on earth, a life amidst the living, a thread stitching us through to those who have come before and to those who will come after. We have gathered here to celebrate both the quilts of antebellum Baltimore and those beautiful Baltimore-style Albums, which surround us here. Stitch by stitch, stepping stone by stepping stone, our

EDIE ZAKEM

contemporaries have taken this quilt style, this mystery, so beautifully beyond Baltimore and out into the rapids of our modern lives. Out of the mystery of those antique quilts we come, and into it we return.

Traditionally, we quiltmakers have stitched our noblest souls, our loftiest commitments into our Albums. Let us believe that a nobly wrought quilt increases the moral wealth of man and enriches the future. "Human destiny," Rev. Robert Cope wrote, in my father's memorial service, "is a great one because the essence of it is tragic. All that we build crumbles. All that we embody turns to dust. All that we love we must one day leave behind us. That which alone endures is the spirit in which we understand and meet our fate. This we pass on to our children, our comrades, our friends. Only a breath indeed, but the breath of life." And for a quiltmaker her testament is tangible. She threads the fabric of her life through with a noble acceptance and love. And she is reassured to know that her quilts are like old friends: They connect her to the past, they give happiness and stability to her present, and through this, her Friendship's Offering, they tie her to the future.

Will the beauty of these quilts on exhibit lie as much in what they hide as what they reveal? Let's braid our three-ply cord of judgment over that one as we proceed now, on to the show.

THANK YOU. AND ENJOY!

INSTITUTIONS like this operate in two ways. While they improve art, they improve the artizan [sic]. While they facilitate and perfect the labor of the hands, they call into action, rouse up and make active, the labor of the brain. And this last is truly their noblest function. The work of the hand … has the common fate of all human creations: but thought is imperishable, and once developed, expressed and illustrated, lives forever.

—John H. B. Latrobe, Esq., "Annual Address before the Maryland Institute for the Promotion of the Mechanic Arts, Delivered at its First Annual Exhibition, Opened at Washington Hall Building, Baltimore, October 1848."

(Endnotes)

1 Spelling in the 19th Century is delightfully inconsistent compared to the present—in family names as well as in fraternal orders. So we find Oddfellows used interchangeably with Odd Fellows, and Rebeccas with Rebekahs.

2 Thomas G. Beharrell, *Odd Fellow Monitor and Guide, History of the Degree of Rebekah, and Its Teachings, Emblems of the Order*, Indianapolis, Robert Douglass, 1882, (www.archive.org). Gentle reader, I feel compelled to correct in this volume, the decades-long misunderstanding I've held concerning the beehive and the dove, those common Rebekah (women Odd Fellows) symbols. The critical point is that in **1851** these were not Rebekah symbols, nor were the women empowered to use Odd Fellow symbols except for their men, until well after the Album Era (High-style 1846–1852) had ended. The 1851 originally noted in the text here honored the hardworking, supportive wives and daughters of Odd Fellows. The "Daughters of Rebekah" degree awarded in 1851 was an honorary degree only. These ladies had obligations as a Ladies' Auxiliary to the Odd Fellows (husbands and fathers) to whom they were related.

But, yes, the BAQs are full of doves and beehives, symbols that post-Album Era, became official Rebekah symbols. The point is that they were potent, well-understood symbols (visible signs of invisible things) since Biblical times. As Biblical symbols, they speak without words in the Albums. But when, as a matter of curiosity, did the Rebekahs gain full Odd Fellow rights? Briefly: In 1868, the state-instituted "Degree Lodges of Rebekah" began in Bloomfield, Iowa, and spread rapidly so that in 1872 all the state Rebekah Degree lodges were elevated to report, as did the men's lodges, to the Odd Fellow Grand Lodge of the United States. In 1886, the Rebekahs became its own distinct organization.

Beharrell's *Odd Fellows' Monitor and Guide* is a delicious pie-slice of 19th Century American history focusing on the Rebekahs, their symbols and degrees. Reading it, you'll sense the Albums' sweet perfume of encouragement towards self-improvement, beneficence in helping others in need; of the teamwork de Tocqueville and so many others have considered an element of the 19th and 20th century American character.

While the symbols' ancient meanings (in The Lexicon) hold true, this book's sequel explores how when we "stitch symbols together into *metaphors*," the skies over old Baltimore's panoramic patterns brighten beatifically! You may be surprised, gentle reader, at how a deeper immersion in Album Era life and times alters dramatically many of 1983's Pattern Notes, reproduced herein. These original Pattern Notes document how far our understanding will have come by the time this book's sequel debuts.

Are Quilts Art? What's It to Us?

Published in an early 1990's *American Quilter Magazine,* this piece was inspired by contentious Letters to the Editor of that journal, letters reacting to an apparently thought-provoking AQS Awards Night Address delivered by professional quiltmaker Michael James. Regrettably, I missed Michael's speech, but the letters' heated tenor set me to weighing the question, "Are Quilts Art?"
— Elly Sienkiewicz

ALBERTINE VEENSTRA

Revival, Reinterpretation, Reproduction, or Art?

ABUZZ these days in the quilt world is a question that won't go away: Are quilts Art? Is it simply a definition of Art we want? Plato defines "Fine Arts" as those concerned with an "attainment of the beautiful." By this, and by several *Webster's* definitions, some quilts, perhaps most, are surely Art. Despite plenty of qualifying definitions, debate continues, suggesting that some quiltmakers want to imply a judgmental pronouncement by labeling certain quilts "Art"—while others resist this. We're in lofty company! "Aesthetics" (the study of beauty) consumed philosophers such as Plato, Hobbes, Burke, and Immanuel Kant. But perhaps there's a warning here, too, not to expect a definitive—one size fits all—answer to the question. Nonetheless a lively exchange of ideas about what we do—make quilts—is fun. Then, too, this debate might even give us more insight into why we love quiltmaking so.

Still, I'm not quite sure what the nature of the interest in this question is. Quilt world concern doesn't really seem to be over the centuries-old Aesthetic Philosophy topics (Beauty as Truth; Beauty and Morality; Beauty as Expression; the Subjectivity of Beauty; etc.). But the matter has definitely got the attention of some quiltmakers—though it's unlikely to affect either anyone's quilts or why they make them. What is all the fuss about? Why does the query rile quiltmakers so? (That question intrigues me even more!) Over the past dozen years, thousands, myself included, have become obsessed with Baltimore-style Album Quilts. With antebellum Baltimores having sold within the past decade for six-figures—prices any painter would be pleased to command—this alone makes it interesting to at least consider an inquiry into when quilts are Art.

Victorian Amish?

WHICH QUILTS, for example, stand the test of time? It seems that some measure of Art must be how it is viewed centuries later. In sculpture, painting, music, architecture, *and quilts*, certain works, certain styles are remembered. Not only do they hold their value, but it increases. Distance counts. Take the catch-all period name, "Victorian": Mid-20th Century, that term was almost an epithet. Currently we feel an affinity for the period, a sense that much about its Art tells us something about ourselves as we, too, cope with rapid social change. Victorian is not really a style. Rather, the Victorian period was a time when multiple styles were in transition. It surprises me that the graphic simplicity of a mid-19th Century Pennsylvania Amish quilt, for instance, is as "Victorian" as the florid overabundance of a similarly vintage-styled Baltimore Album Quilt.

Album Quilts, like Albums of all sorts, are collections on a theme. The inclusion in a quilter's Album of diverse elements—of neo-classic ornament, of mementos of significant events in her lifetime, of friendships, fraternity, patriotism, and religion, of nature's bounty, and of the Industrial Revolution's powerful reflections—made the collection rich. For a quiltmaker, it must have been a particularly inviting period. The challenge was to stitch this diversity into an artistic whole. A beautiful Album is not an easy quilt to design: Some are much more artistic than others. The antique Albums showcase lots of different sets and borders. Certain Baltimore Album Quilt sets are repeated, but even with some repetition, the style's scope was phenomenally rich: By its breadth, we see that it struggled. The most successful quilts in the genre prove Owen Jones' thesis that Art is "best when it struggles."

Art is best when it struggles

THE DRAWING to a close of the 20th Century really does invite a thoughtful look backward. A good place to start on the question *Are quilts Art?* is by listening to a bit of the same discussion from the last century.

The Englishman Owen Jones (1806–1889) was an architect, designer, and teacher of Applied Arts at the South Kensington School of Design. In his *The Grammar of Ornament* (1856) he voiced concern that the Age's excessive use of historic and exotic styles was becoming muddled and cloying. Because some of Jones's principles inspired the Arts and Crafts Movement, certain of his ideas on Art are relevant to our consideration of "quilts as Art." Jones believed "the western world too often settled for the simple copying of exotic ornament and sensational effect in every field of Art. . . . [His] strong conviction was that historical and exotic styles should be used as sources primarily of inspiration rather than for imitation." He insisted "on honesty to one's materials and on soundness of craftsmanship—in short, on Artistic integrity." (*The Grammar of Ornament*, 1986 reprint, Crown Publishers, Inc., NY)

Jones cautions that we need to "ascertain . . . the peculiar circumstances which rendered an ornament beautiful, because it was appropriate." He was convinced "that the future progress of Ornamental Art may be best secured by engrafting on the experience of the past, the knowledge we may obtain by a return to Nature for fresh inspiration." Thus, among Album-makers, a fresh look in our gardens—at ferns and flowers, buds and leaves—has inspired a new dimensionality in appliqué. This in turn has led the Album style off in directions now definably "beyond Baltimore."

"To attempt to build up theories of Art, or to form a style, independently of the past, would be an act of supreme folly," he continues. "It would be at once to reject the experiences and accumulated knowledge of thousands of years. On the contrary, we should regard as our inheritance all the successful labors of the past, not blindly following them, but employing them simply as guides to find the true path."

"When Art struggles," Jones concludes, "it succeeds; when reveling in its own successes, it as signally fails. The pleasure we receive in contemplating the rude attempts at ornament of the most savage tribes arises from our appreciation of a difficulty accomplished;

we are at once charmed by the evidence of the intention and surprised at the simple and ingenious process by which the result is obtained. In fact, what we seek in every work of "Art," whether it be humble or pretentious, is the evidence of mind, the evidence of that desire to create. . ., and which all, feeling a natural instinct within them, are satisfied with when they find it developed in others. It is strange, but so it is, that this evidence of mind will be more readily found in the rude attempts at ornament of a savage tribe than in the innumerable productions of a highly-advanced civilization."

ROSALYNN MCKOWN

The Industrial Revolution cast Art and Craft in new light

MASS-PRODUCED Chinese quilts come to mind when we read the next Owen Jones principle of Art: "Individuality decreases in the ratio of the power of production. When Art is manufactured by combined effort, not originated by individual effort, we fail to recognize *those true instincts which constitute its greatest charm.*"

Mass-produced articles made possible by the Industrial Revolution, for example, must at first have thrilled consumers. Fairly quickly, though, the more individual beauty of the handmade regained favor. Speaking out against commercialism, Owen Jones, John Ruskin, and William Morris advocated natural decoration, pure color, and production by hand work. Their ideas inspired a movement, the Arts and Crafts Movement, whose reverence for handwork we share. Are we trying again to define the work of our hand here at another century's end, here in "the Post-Industrial Age"? It seems worth following the evolution, the accumulated "history" of Art to help us answer our quilt/Art question. For to some extent, Art, like the Law, becomes defined by precedent. At minimum, the perception of what Art is, has to be open to changes caused by science and technology

"There's one name that is threaded through the recounting of my own little BAQ journey. It is Elly; artist, teacher, scholar, and friend, who introduced so many of us to the Baltimores and who keeps us at it."

—Rosalynn McKown

as much as by change caused by politics or religion.

Guardians of the Culture

FAITHFUL reproduction of old masters has been a time-honored way of learning Art, from ancient China to traditional Western Art instruction. Familiarization by repetition seems the surest way to learn all that a classic painting or quilt has to teach. If it actually "looks the same," we've learned a phenomenal amount. Perhaps that was our goal: to copy a great work so that we can internalize its principles and techniques. Can a piece of Art be an exquisite copy? So exquisite that it becomes "a fraud"?

Nothing upsets the "Guardians of the Culture," the judges of Art, the "Art world," quite so much as to be taken in by a fraud. But that may be because falling for a fraud says that your powers of discernment—your "expertise"—aren't what you'd like us all to believe they are. Unless they are modest by nature, or make an effort at modesty, media age guardians of the culture can easily set off on a power trip. Are Guardians of the Culture surfacing in the quilt world, here at the end of the 20th Century? It's something to think about. And perhaps something to be on our guard against.

So many, myself (fleeing Art academia) included, were drawn to quiltmaking's folk art. Its tradition seemed to invite us with open arms. To me, quiltmaking implied that there are no rights, no wrongs, no judgmental calls to clip your wings. My feeling about quilts said, your quilts are valid because you make them. And when one of your quilts feels exceptional to you, by definition, it is. Old judge's catalogues, recently unearthed at the Library of Congress, show, however, that even in the 19th Century, quilt show judging was an important factor in advancing the art. While no quiltmaker is forced to enter a competition, for many the time comes when they invite judgment. So quiltmaking embraces both free spirits and those who thrive on their culture's commendation. I think we all like it this way, cherish its freedom.

Faithful Reproduction or Fraud?

TO MY KNOWLEDGE, no quiltmaker has ever faithfully reproduced an old quilt with intent to misrepresent, trick, or deceive. So to date in contemporary quiltmaking, Fraud is no issue. In fact, our quiltmaking tradition encourages not only learning by reproduction, but preserving and passing the culture on thereby. But nonetheless, can a work of Art be a copy? There is almost universal agreement that exact copies are not Art; they're copies. In American quiltmaking, though, they seem something more: high craft at the very least; but still more: high tribute laboriously paid to a common American Culture. This is important, for it may explain somewhat, why such strong feelings are aroused by even the suggestion that to dub a quilt High Craft, "Art Needlework," or perhaps Folk Art is somehow to value it less than to label it with the seal of approval—the term, "Art."

Quiltmaking: Part of the global popularity of America

AMONG quiltmakers the time-honored tradition of "plain and fancy" endures. Even when "utilitarian," or "quick 'n' easy," or "whizzy-whacker" quilts are made, the very act of their making may, to the quiltmaker, be a ritual participation in communal American culture, both past and present. (We know quiltmaking today is born neither of practical necessity, nor a desire to economize. It is perceived as a worthy investment of time and money. It is viewed as a medium for self-expression, even as a bid for an earthly immortality.) We shouldn't trivialize something which means so much.

These simple quilts are given (a gift of oneself) to loved ones, and their making is regularly shared in classes or at quilt guild show 'n' tells. They are the tissue which connects us to family, friends, fellow-quiltmakers. They establish our belonging to the group. Perhaps it is specifically this ritual aspect to what was

MARA WARWICK

perceived initially as "American" quiltmaking, which also draws women from other nations, some with quilting antecedents of their own, as to a magnet.

We all recognize our growing interdependence: the globalization of our economics, and even of our increasingly diverse society. Quiltmaking's ritual may be a gentle, intuitive way of finding fellowship, even with quiltmakers of foreign tongue. The quilt world crosses barriers: age barriers, economic barriers, racial barriers, professional barriers, even nation-state barriers. There is uncertainty and discomfort, both here and abroad, about the "new internationalism." Quiltmaking, however, provides a small and tentative way to stitch the world together. The individual quiltmaker's passion still attaches most ardently to her more intimate world: to her nation, her community, her family; and this, too, is healing. For while quiltmaking's current international popularity seemed to stem originally from its identification with American culture—like Coke® or blue jeans—once any woman begins quiltmaking's journey, it reaffirms who she is, and from whence she comes.

Individualism in the US, along with communitarianism

HISTORICALLY, the mainstream of American quiltmaking seems to have been rooted in self-expression, but also communal expression. The artist-quiltmaker's vision is inseparable from her sense of belonging to, and being grateful and beholden to her community. Even our mythology of quilting pioneer women recalls their stitching symbolic cloth, color, or pattern into quilts, longing to reinforce connections to the people and place from which they've come. Debate over an approved standard of quilts as Art often seems to lose sight of this fundamental truth. Current definitions of quilts as Art would seem to emphasize the individual's self-[centered] expression,

not the expression of an individual's ardent yearning to reaffirm a place in communal culture. This seems par for the course. For while counter-cultural—and by definition highly individualistic—manifestations are present in all liberal Western societies today, the great art of the Renaissance, for example, was so often based on the Catholic faith.

Quiltmaking, the Quilt World, it seems to me, has tended to harbor a more communitarian view. Many U.S. quiltmakers not only preserve American communal culture, they feel a living connection to it through quiltmaking's ritual. Were quiltmakers not so intent upon strengthening the ties that bind, rather than exacerbating those that divide, the question might now arise: Must one be more than an Artist to be a Quiltmaker? We first need to think about what standards the term "Art" should imply.

The Emperor's New Clothes

DO PEOPLE always recognize a work of Art? Can a teacher, for example, completely overlook genius in a student? Can Art be described? Or must one feel, "That is brilliant, it speaks to me"? Several incidents I've come across recently suggest that some "Guardians of Culture," the judges of Art, may finally feel that they are being had, sense that they may have been duped, like the emperor by the tailors. In *The Washington Times* of July 4th, 1993, R. Emmett Tyrrell, Jr. comments on the "muttering in the Art world." He notes that "From Italy comes word that the Venice '*Biennale*' has been a bust. . . . The '*Biennale*' is the world's most celebrated international Art assemblage. On the scene, the *New York Times* reports, 'The disappointment was palpable and widespread.' There were piles of rocks that somehow failed to stir the spirit. The *Times* produced a picture of what looked like a primitive dollhouse. . . . It too failed to impress. And there was drivel framed, rubbish mounted. . . . All of it aroused a vague yearning in some of the more astute critics for that long-forgotten talent 'painting.'"

What the Art world's Guardians of Culture are being handed is meant to astound: It

"The traditional Baltimore album quilts inspire me, but at the same time they welcome me to integrate my individual creativity."

—Anne Carter

YOLANDA (YOLY) TOVAR

"The needle worker uses appliqué with a symbolic language so that through needle, thread, and fabric, she can represent her ideas, her dreams, her aspirations. She creates a world of beauty that catches a moment in time, one preserved for prosperity by the appliqué design."

—Yolanda "Yoly" Tovar

trades on the coins of shock and novelty but not even craft. What begins to be felt is that Art must meet some standard; that it must at minimum be high craft. It must have some element of magic and that magic must be visible to the audience. What has passed for Art has often been only novelty. In fact I wonder if pure novelty can ever be great Art, since great Art must interpret some part of the culture in which it is embedded. It must tell us something important about ourselves.

The "Smithsonian Quilts"

THAT'S YOUR Smithsonian question, then: Universally and generically, copies are not Art, they are copies. There's no magic there. These commercial reproductions don't even reflect high craft, a point which does offend quiltmakers who take pride in their fine stitches. One of Owen Jones's precepts addresses the "Art" of copied quilts: "The principles discoverable in the works of the past belong to us, not so the results. It is taking the ends for the means."

Does Art need a prophetic voice, something original? What is the motivation for Art, or in this case, for the quilts? Commerce is an honorable endeavor, but people engaged in commerce don't normally produce great Art—not even stateside quiltmakers who generate quilts commercially, not usually even quiltmakers who regularly create art commercially. They may produce pleasing products, but the inner search that an Art-

ist undertakes in producing Art can easily be overtaken by an outer search: What will the public buy? Or, what will win the contest? Even Picasso, notes Mr. Tyrrell, "gave up serious painting for the easy buck." An Artist who is "recognized" is in danger of losing his soul. Not only today, but always. He is fawned over, hauled around as an honored guest, "well fed" to the extent that he loses the hunger that wrenched the Art from his soul.

Like quiltmaking, Art must be grounded in the culture

BY WHAT sort of standards should we define Art? One standard might be that at minimum it be high craft, that it is hard work, effort, skill. (Or, as in a Zen monk's paintings: hard work, effort, and skill have led to the seemingly instantaneous portrayal of insight.) Another might be that it must have some large measure of the Artist in it (not a monkey playing with paints and an easel) and that some large part of the magic be conveyed to the audience. And perhaps that prevents pure novelty from ever being great Art, because Art must somehow be grounded in the culture. For a quilt to be great Art, it may need to bring something significant from the past. It has also been suggested that for a work of Art to have future meaning, it must trade on the coin of its own time, must use currency of the present.

The quilt world still imposes standards when judging quilts. Unlike the jury for the *Biennale,* some quilt judges may tend to err in the other direction: sometimes valuing quantifiable qualities (straightness of binding, how the corners align when the quilt is folded) more than its unquantifiable qualities. Exceptionalism in the latter has marked those quilts which have, more than a century later, ended up in Art museums or being traded at auction for six figure prices. Thus the *'Biennale'* scenario is not likely to happen soon at a Quilt Symposium show. But I've seen it happen in the hands of Art Museums where 'Guardians of the Culture' placed highest value on novelty and sensational effect.

Reinterpretation of a Classic Style

ALMOST without exception, shock value quilts (or novelty quilts with no apparent gift from the past) have a moment's notoriety, then are never seen again. They tend not to have holding power, tend to be too transient a contribution to America's cultural stream to make a lasting mark. By contrast, occasionally an old quilt style or technique, perhaps one that has slipped almost beyond memory, inspires a seemingly novel concept. When the new quilt presents this concept with such clarity as to be readily intelligible and repeatable, it may cause a revival of proportions which will surely be noticed in our culture's history. Then one grand new quilt may spawn intense investigations by many quiltmakers, so that a genre of quilts is revived so vividly that it, too, becomes a single strand in the twist of styles that ties our century to the one before it and to the one after it.

Had more quilts survived from the 18th Century, I'm convinced we'd see a longer history of traceable quiltmaking style-cycles. A propos quilt-style cycles, Owen Jones asserts "that the modifications and developments which have taken place from one style to another have been caused by a sudden throwing off of some fixed trammel, which set thought free for a time, till the new idea, like the old became again fixed, to give birth in its turn to fresh inventions."

We recognize the truism: "New" sells. "New" interests us in fashions and in quilts. It is the innovative spin to the old and familiar which catches our eye at the quilt show. Sometimes we can look back and see when and where a quilt trend started. "One of life's most fulfilling moments," writes Edward B. Lindaman (*Thinking in Future Tense*, 1978), "occurs in that split second when the familiar is suddenly transformed into the dazzling aura of the profoundly new. . . . These breakthroughs are too infrequent, more uncommon than common; and we are mired most of the time in the mundane and the trivial. The shocker: what seems mundane and trivial is the very stuff that discovery is made of. The

only difference is our perspective, our readiness to put the pieces together in an entirely new way and to see patterns where only shadows appeared just a moment before."

Thus, "from time to time a mind stronger than those around will impress itself on a generation," explains Owen Jones, "and carry with it a host of others of less power following the same track, yet never so closely as to destroy the individual ambition to create; hence the cause of styles, and of the modification of styles."

Quilt styles, too, proliferate. Since early on in this quilt revival, by the hands of quiltmakers Nancy Crow and Michael James, and later, through Alison Goss and Carol Fallert, strip piecing expanded from the antique string-quilt concept to something so vividly changed as to be quite new again. So, too, pieced Heirloom Medallion quilts became once again the stuff of dreams inspired anew by Jinny Beyer. Then through Judy Mathieson old stars were reborn in a blaze of glory, and Jean Ray Laury revived the Victorian stenciled quilt—with a box of modern paints, transfers, and a smile! Crazy quilts' eclectic elegance now reflects modern lives, influenced by Judith Montano. Similarly, landscape quilts, rare in the past, are worked on brilliantly fresh canvases by Nancy Halpern, Jean Johnson, and Joen Wolfrom. Nancy Pearson's exquisite flowers recalled quiltmaking's last revival, then appliquéd it to the present. Sewing machine work, too, has, in the hands of Harriet Hargraves and Deborah Wagner, finally been brought back to its late Victorian era throne—only now the Princess has become a Queen. And thus quiltmaking's barque sails proudly on, soon to crest another century. Which of these quilts will history single out as great? Only time will tell.

Are quilts Art? What's it to us?

ARE QUILTS ART (with a capital "A")? The short answer is: Some are, some aren't. Moreover, the answer as to which is which probably can't be decided until after we're gone. Art endures. To a large extent, only when

"While fulfilling the need I believe all women have to create beauty in their world, through the album blocks, they were able to interpret what was happening around them at the time. From the beauty of a bird in a tree in their back yard, to the new monument erected in memory of some event, to the spiritual world of faith, hope, and love, their lives are there for us to see. As I stitch these blocks, I form a connection in my mind with these talented women."

—Sandra Reynolds

SUSAN MARIE BRYAN

we're history, will a judgment be made as to which quilts are Art. Which quilt styles were only flashes in the pan? (Those latter, we hope will nestle safely, treasured by their families, for each was art to the one who made it.)

My Album Quilt obsession has led me to haunt old cemeteries. They may hold a clue to the query, "What's it to us?" I seek out graveyards with obelisks, for these are the right vintage for Album symbols. There, I've noticed the same emblems on tombstones that occur in the Baltimore Album Quilts. Interesting. Those Victorian symbols seem to speak predominantly of communitarianism, of the faith and other membership groups by which one defines oneself and to whom one has "plighted one's troth." By the present era, though, group insignias become more rare. In Barre, Vermont, home of Rock of Ages Monument Company, Hope Cemetery is a sculpture garden where among others, the stonecutters have buried their own. There is a wealth of modern symbols on the grave markers, but they seem to have evolved to reflect someone seen more as an isolated individual than as a member of a group: There, symbols of sports, recreations, occupations, and pictures of faces and even of modern residences, mingle with frequency among other graves marked by religious emblems or no insignia at all.

The uniquely modern symbols seem to say, "This was me, this is who I was. This is what I loved, this is where my spirit lives." At first, I didn't know what to make of these modern symbols. They surprised and puzzled me. But it shouldn't be so surprising: Individualism is as strong in American Culture as communalism. Historically those forces are always in contention. Here, the individualistic thread may be more powerful than in any society on earth, while the communal thread has historically been strong as well.

Perhaps this is the answer to "What's it to us?" In quiltmaking, it is as in all else in this land of powerful opposites. The individualistic thread wants to say, "*My* quilts are Art. They are more than quilts, more than folk Art, more than high craft. They express who I am, what I love, where my soul lives. They

may express what angers me, what I hate, what I would change. They express my unique vision, they sing with a voice that is not the common voice. But by their magic, they will affect the viewer, make him hear my song."

The communitarian thread wants, perhaps, to say, "By this quilt I am a living part of a continuum. I want this work of my hands to extol our common culture, to give it present and renewed life, to pass quiltmaking's traditions on. I want to give the love my quilt conveys tangible form: to blanket my home with it; gift family and friends with it; commemorate the Album of my life with it, leave it as a living testament of me and the community of which I am a part."

Even in this age, we have the old conflict (present from the beginning of American history): insistent individualism versus communitarianism—and the song plays on, even here in our quilt world. And for some unfathomable reason, I find that extraordinarily comforting! Those who want to define some quilts as Art will do so. And those who want to hold the threads that bind will hold on tight. Yes, of course this question matters to us. But let's not get all hot and bothered about it. We live in the Land of the Free. In quiltmaking still, we can do whatever we jolly well please.

Baltimore Beauties as a series ends now. That, too, gives us an excuse for taking stock, for asking if these Albums we make are Art. *Volume III, Papercuts and Plenty,* is my ninth book now (including 1983's *Spoken Without a Word*), which, with patterns and techniques, teaches the expressive style of the classic Baltimore Albums. The neo-Baltimores now being made, are more *revivalist and reinterpretive*—a revival of both the style but also of the style's invitation to expression—than faithful *reproductions* of the old. The enthusiasm with which these quilts are being made, speaks to how gratifying they are. Are these quilts Art? Time will tell if some are, some aren't. Certainly all intend to be. Certainly all, in their maker's eye, meet Owen Jones's criterion that "True beauty results from that repose which the mind feels when the eye, the intellect, and the affections, are satisfied from the absence of want."

And besides, What's it to anyone, more than to you or I who made the quilt?

The Baltimore Album Legacy, Briefly

Elly Sienkiewicz opened the Second Baltimore Album Revival Quilt Exhibition and Contest with the following remarks.

ARTISTS *have to forge a character subtle enough to nourish and protect and foster the growth of the part of themselves that makes art, and at the same time practical enough to deal with the world pragmatically. They have to maintain a position between care of themselves and care of their work in the world . . .*

—Anne Truitt,
*Daybook, The
Journal of An Artist*

AUTHOR'S NOTE:
Today's younger quilt-making women most often say, "I like hand appliqué because it's portable. I can stitch at meetings, or while I'm waiting to pick up my children. I can do it in the evening and be with my family."

THE BALTIMORE ALBUM STYLE is complex, one that has immediate visual impact, while richly rewarding closer inspection. The most opulent classic Baltimore Album Quilts raise questions, have an air of mystery, and arouse such compelling curiosity that we must investigate diverse roads of inquiry. This tension enlightens us, not in the modern way of pat answers and data-based arguments, but in a transcendent way, one that leaves us open to broader understandings.

The fanciest antebellum Baltimores dazzle with lifelike draftsmanship, evocative fabric, and half-forgotten iconographies. The mid-19th century's ornate Baltimore Album Quilt style might have been an historic flash of genius, but became instead a classic. Its popularity bespeaks a movement, one which flourished for a decade or so in Baltimore, then spread far north and west of the city which had spawned it. We moderns inherited hundreds of related Album Quilts—all so mysterious in origin, each so fascinating in feature. In a little-analyzed reincarnation, this style is now born again in the late 20th century. It has taken wider hold than its ancestor, gaining followers to the north in Canada; east to European capitals, on to American expatriates in Saudi Arabia, and further to Japan and Korea; south to South Africa, Australia, and New Zealand. Now, in the second decade of this revival, Baltimore style has developed its own recognizably late-20th-century characteristics. We call this contemporary-style Album Quilt a "Revivalist Baltimore."

Confluent forces shaped Revivalist Baltimores. Back in 1983, *Spoken Without a Word* initially met the challenge by reproducing antique Baltimore block patterns and probing the secrets of their symbols. By the publication of *Baltimore Beauties and Beyond, Volume I* (1989), it was more than enough simply to rediscover the basics of stitching classic Baltimore Album style appliqué. There, large-scale prints are often paired with papercut appliqués. This initially was an innovative practice, but now characterizes Revivalist Baltimores. Because the Album style offered a challenge and satisfied a hunger, it caught on. *Dimensional Appliqué* (1994), for example, firmly inserted ribbon into the changing style. As the *Baltimore Beauties* series grew, so did communal knowledge of the style. The women and times that had cradled the original Album Quilts became familiar. As was the case for women of that era, the winds of political and social change leave us feeling less in control of our lives. We discover an affinity: the more we understand those ladies, the better we understand ourselves. These sensibilities coupled with our burgeoning mastery of appliqué have set us free. It is as though we moderns are admiring daughters, come finally into our own womanhood. Emulating our "mothers," we stitch our own lives into expressive Album Quilts, proudly evoking their heritage. Occasionally a modern Album is so reminiscent of an elder that it brings tears to the eyes, as though a classic quilt has been reborn through a living soul. At other times, only we who know and love the old one can detect the family's genes in a Revivalist Album, so different does the new one look.

Enjoined to compose an essay for *Baltimore Album Legacy*, I considered summarizing this renaissance. To be frank, though, I have no desire to name an epoch come and gone, for it is but newly in full bloom. Too many love, too much, the path "Baltimore" has set them on; find the Baltimore style too vital, too suited to our own lives here in the late 20th century, too fascinating and all-encompassing not to continue on where this journey leads them. Beginning Baltimore classes fill across the country while some, long on this journey and stitching on their "Baltimore" intermittently, savor its evolution. Rare women (Marian Brockschmidt, Cleda Dawson, Ardeth Laake, and Nancy Welsch among them) have made six and more intricate "Baltimores." Some stitch their second or third Revivalist Album, while others make one square at a time, enjoying the process and in no hurry to finish. In public forums, Revivalist Baltimores—each more compelling than

YOLANDA (YOLY) TOVAR

AUTHOR'S NOTE:
Can quilting be meditation?

the last—have in recent years taken top prize at the world's most prestigious quilt competitions. This bespeaks an appreciative public and a current fluency in stitchery techniques and symbolic tongues.

The Baltimore Revival raises questions whose answers one can only intuit: Why are Baltimore-style Album Quilts born again—now? In what ways does getting to know the Classic Baltimores nourish us? What loneliness or longing does it lessen? Might Revivalist Album Quiltmaking serve a connective function? (It connects Album makers into a recognizable sub-culture as much as it connects Album quilters from one century to the next. It integrates the quiltmaker's life as she recalls loved ones, records memories, and selects meaningful inscriptions. It helps us comprehend life's mysteries, answer unanswerable questions, work out contradictions which haunt us. Its ritual takes one on a transformational journey.) Much is said these days about attending to our spiritual needs. Is Album-making in part a spiritual activity? This Exhibition's visual feast will provide some answers. In addition, this catalog's written selections address our wonderment in an experiential manner. First, the "Author's Underlinings and Marginalia" traces my own fascination with pondering these matters. The second excerpt is from my journal after I'd spent the day judging a major international quilt show. In the *art spirit*, may this writing

blend with the images of Album Quilts on exhibition. In the words of Robert Henri, the art spirit's "subject is beauty—or happiness, and man's approach to it is various."

Passion . . . These Are the Quilts that Make You Cry

To judge a major quilt show is an honor. It is also a responsibility borne seriously. And it is hard work. Yesterday I judged such a show and upon returning, fell asleep in my hotel room without a pause for supper. Tomorrow, I will walk over to the George R. Brown center and in the Quilt Festival Office there, sign those American International Quilt Guild prize ribbons which I have awarded. Tonight I am sitting on my window balcony beside the sixth floor pool deck of the Hyatt Regency. The air is a tease, dancing with my scarf and patting my cheeks, pushing at my hair, and riffling the water. Ceaseless bar music plays over the October-empty pool: the sound is seamless and a bit too loud. But its throb is exhilarating, like city lights and crowds of people moving as though on mechanical sidewalks, at rush hour. The light here is unfamiliar: low floodlights set the occasional landscaped tree aglow. Cottony clouds reflect the nighttime city's pinkish aura and slip by, moving almost imperceptibly against the charcoaled sky. Strings of diamond-bright lights draw electric building outlines, while here and there a window glows warm yellow through billowing drapes.

It is after dark, yet the night is alive with unfamiliar lights and sounds. And I am a bit lonely, a solitary quilter come to an international quilt gathering halfway across the country. This elegant hotel is a hollow stack of guest floors with a sunken lounge in the center; a trio is now playing beside the bar and cocktail waitresses attend the throng of guests. Though I would surely know some people there, I shied away at the thought of entering that crowd alone and have instead come to sit awhile in the cool, in the dark, by the pool. "Excuse me, ma'am," says the young man whom I'd noticed out of the corner of my eye. He is the deck's other sole occupant, taking a smoke and an evening walk. "Were you out here last night? That building over there was all lit up with green and red neon lights. It was so pretty. I wondered what it was." I answer in a friendly, but older-lady-cautious way. He is a solidly built tow-head, clean-shaven and in his twenties. In the dark his black and white striped jersey is more visible than his face. He has moved on, but I sensed that he was lonely, too, as we are wont to be when we are away from home.

I am thinking now of the quilt show, of the lives stitched into those quilts, of the degree of intimacy revealed, or of the feelings hardly touched upon. Some quilts were light-hearted and quick, others were intellectual and almost art-school perfect. But certain quilts held you as though in communion with another soul. In their stillness, they spoke: one could feel echoed the still, sad music of humanity. But more; for some rare quilts offered the gift of a life full enough with hard-come-by faith to share wisdom with another fellow; to share it even with a generation yet unborn. I don't really mean a rote religious faith or even necessarily something one can put into words. One senses that faith of someone who has lived life deeply, who has seen its dark side, but who never falters in putting life's puzzle pieces into a positive picture.

We were four judges for four hundred quilts. Our day had begun with a 7:15 a.m. breakfast. The quilts were divided into categories so that each judge looked at some one hundred quilts. A scribe assisted each one of us, recording our careful comments quilt by quilt, then, as they were completed, taking each judge's top prize winners to the head scribe. By 4:00 p.m. we congregated to choose the Best of Show large quilt and the Best of Show small quilt from among the first prize winners in each category. The convention center was almost empty now, save for us judges and the four hundred quilts. Tomorrow it would be a hive of activity generated by the merchants and manufacturers setting up for Quilt Market, the quilt world's wholesale show. By next week's end, more than 50,000 people are expected to have come to see the quilts. Gratefully, we accepted the offer to be driven on a golf cart to review the rows of quilts. Each judge pointed out the top winner for her categories. The small quilt Best of Show was quickly agreed upon: It was a fiber art piece, exceptionally well done.

By sheer number, competition was stiffer among the large quilts, for a large quilt may require more of the self than a small quilt, and the sheer magnitude of effort may result in a higher achievement. Our final choice was not easy, but the comments that led up to it were revealing. The top prize winners seemed of two characters: On the one hand, they were stunning quilts, quilts embodying an idea conceived and carefully worked out in colored cloth, painstakingly arranged, then carefully stitched through with patterned quilting. The level of art throughout the show was breathtaking, as though world-class museum treasures had nothing on these modern quilt-makers' talent, creativity, diligence, and high standards. On the other hand, there were quilts perhaps a tad less perfectly wrought in quantifiable ways, yet they took one's breath away. This second group of top contenders had some quality much harder to name.

One judge said, "Those other quilts are perfect designs, fabric art, intellectual triumphs. But these two are the kind of quilt that makes you cry." We had, all four, come back finally to one of the two. It was an Album

To *know what you prefer instead of humbly saying Amen to what the world tells you you ought to prefer, is to have kept your soul alive.*

—Robert Louis Stevenson

WHAT *we play is life.*
—Louis Armstrong

WHAT *is all this juice and all this joy?*
—Gerard Manley Hopkins (1844–89)

AS *to me, I know of nothing else but miracles.*
—Walt Whitman

WALT *Whitman's work is an autobiography—not of haps and mishaps, but of his deepest thought, his life indeed.*
—Robert Henri

AUTHOR'S NOTE:
Each hard-wrought quilt is an autobiography. But it is in the very nature of Revivalist Baltimores to specifically **intend** *autobiography.*

GENA HOLLAND

Quilt, softly colored, yet lively and full of the stuff of life: Tiny bell-shaped blossoms hung on fragile stems, a life-size ladybug crawled up a stem to peek into a bud, a maternal blue bird alighted on her nest. And cradled by that bordering generosity of nature were man's ancient offerings of music from a lyre, and woven baskets to hold the blessings and the wonder. Though only nine blocks, each sang such a song of silent praise as to lift the hearts of we beholders.

One of my fellow judges laughed gently to herself. "Yes, this one's clearly it. It will be good to see it pulled out from the others and shown in the light, focused upon as it deserves. Everyone will say 'Elly had such power that a Baltimore-style Album has won 'the Best of Show,' but this quilt is simply the winner.'"

"No." I heard myself saying softly, "It is the quilt. You can feel the maker's passion. This is the kind of quilt that makes you want to cry."

Each judge is allowed a ribbon to give for whatever reason she chooses. I gave my judge's choice ribbon to a beautifully unique quilt called *Ancient Stories*. From dramatically saturated batiks, aboriginal figures and symbols had been reverse appliquéd in a hotly colored primitive dance. The appliqué was neatly done by hand: one could feel the maker's pleasure in it. She chose deep, emphatic lines of machine quilting as the perfect finish, stitching ancient to modern firmly, and with a flourish. I would love to have that quilt, to own it: I liked its aesthetics, I like that it ties us to what has made us what we are. It is an object of art which speaks to me and breaks a smile from my soul. As for the Best of Show quilt, I would love just to hug its maker, for through her beautiful quilt, she shared the gift of her own faith and hope and love. It seemed a gift shyly, but freely, given to we who viewed her quilt. Now I have her gift for all my days of joy and sorrow. Thank you, Ellen Heck. I'll turn in now, knowing that I'll face tomorrow's challenges with courage renewed.

Elly's 2003 Silver Star Address

Source Notes: For one brief slice of quilt history, now passed, "The Silver Star Award" from Karey Bresenhan's International Quilt Festival, Inc. was a commemorative award presented "To one whose work and influence has made—and continues to make—a sizable and positive impact on the quilting industry and community." I was touched to have received this award's honor in 2003. In the autumn of that year, I was to provide a retrospective of a dozen or so of my quilts for exhibition at Karey Bresenhan's Quilts Inc.'s Market and Festival in Houston. I was also to give a Silver Star Award Dinner Address regarding my professional work. That address follows.

The Author's Silver Star Pin. For a time, the International Quilt Festival honored select quilt industry leaders with The Sliver Star Award symbolized by a custom-designed pin in the honoree's style. This is mine in Baltimore style with garnets, my birthstones, and the basket's top bloom, a silver star. *Photo courtesy of the author.*

TONIGHT, I'LL TALK ABOUT GIFTS: How I got here and who I have to thank for it, the gifts of appliqué and Album Quilts, and what our own gifts may give the future.

How did I become a quilter? The short answer is by telephone. It was 39 years ago; I lived in our nation's capital and learned from my Great Great Aunt Atha who lived on Purgatory Run, Alma, in West Virginia. All my life my family has visited the family farm and the West Virginia relatives. There, quilts and quiltlore slipped into my soul. When my second son Alex was on his way, I decided to teach myself to quilt and phoned Aunt Atha with my questions. I hand-pieced an "Evening Star" block, finished it into a pillow, and took it proudly to show her.

"Wee'll El'ner," she began, "It's a piller. And I ain't never put much stock in pillers. You make nine pillers and you got a quilt. And El'ner, a quilt's worth more than pillers!"

My grandmother, May Davina, failing to teach me to read at age four, threaded a needle with color and taught me instead to do embroidery stitches—the fascinating French knot and the draw-anything chain stitch. Sewing's magic though came through my artist mother, Eileen Mary, and she is the artist in me. I was five when she asked me an astonishing question. From an old wool sweater, she would make my sister and me each a hat. "El, what would you like on your hat?" she asked. I must have said trees . . . birds . . . flowers— for that is what I got. Amazing. What power her needle had! From that day on I longed for

needlecraft. That love has led to quiltmaking and the quiltmaking has led to appliqué.

On the strength of that first piller, I hung out my Quilting shingle and started to teach from home. Back then, it was that easy! My first class went on to make Sampler Quilts. Samplers, we know, are a kind of Album Quilt. Like all albums—photograph, record, or stamp albums—an Album Quilt holds a collection of blocks, largely appliquéd, on a theme. But let's talk about Appliqué.

Appliquérs. Such an awkward word for those who apply one decorative layer of cloth to another. They speak of themselves almost as a subculture. What's a subculture? A WSJ opinion piece suggested three characteristics: 1) a charismatic leader, 2) an annual watering hole, and 3) regalia—some article by which members recognize one another. Quilters, I think, clearly qualify. Tonight we gather with our charismatic leader, Karey, at our favorite watering hole, Quilt Festival, and we all recognize the regalia: quilt pins, totebags, and patchwork vests.

Appliquérs may qualify as a subculture. Charismatic leaders? We have lots of them. Annual Watering holes? There's the Appliqué Society, the Baltimore Appliqué Society and The Elly Sienkiewicz Appliqué Academy. Regalia? Perhaps it's our block carriers? Sometimes pizza boxes. Or simply the appliquéd squares within?

Why do we now call ourselves Appliquérs instead of simply Quilters? Could it be because appliqué has more steps than piecing or quilting, and thus has more ritual? We're told that women love ritual. Needleturn appliqué, the art of turning the seam under just before you stitch it, is a bit complicated, asks more of you. By the time you've mastered a sharp point, a clean inside corner, a smooth curve, appliqué may well have slipped into your soul.

Appliquérs speak of their stitching with something akin to reverence. So recent scientific data, which of course pleased us, affirmed that stitching reduces stress and lowers blood

MARY KIEFER BEALS

"I am privileged to be a part of the BAQ Revival. It is an honor to be part of history for women of the future."
—Karen Moraal

pressure. Appliqué also focuses the mind and salves the soul. It seems that as one appliqués, she also changes. The longer she stays on that journey, going into herself for inspiration and out again to listen to what the design wants to become, the longer she stitches, the more something new evolves within her. This care of the soul through stitching is no new idea. Listen to advice stitched on an antique sampler:

While you, my dear, your needlework attend
Observe the counsel of a faithful friend
And strive an inward ornament to gain
Or all your needlework shall prove in vain.

The most famous appliquéd quilts are the Classic Baltimore Albums of the mid-19th century. Their old Album blocks are often symbolic. A symbol, as you know, is a visible sign of something invisible—often an abstract idea like courage (symbolized by a laurel wreath) or Love (symbolized, we all know, by a heart.) Symbols are potent transmitters of lots of information. This use of symbols was the great eye opener for me as I began my Album journey. These quilts were using symbols to speak to us without words. With this discovery, we've recognized the old album quilts as virtual history books, or at "least letters to the present" telling us about

the makers' hopes and beliefs, and about the times and places in which they lived.

Baltimores have earned the title "Classic." You and I call classic something that "sets a standard for all time." We feel a greatness—and a magic in the presence of something human—done superbly well. The harder something is to accomplish, the more we are gratified to witness accomplishment at that pinnacle. Albums are a hard style to work in. All those different blocks to set pleasingly together! You must wrestle with the style's complexity, persist until a thing of beauty takes form.

I met my first old Baltimores hung at a museum in 1982. A young mother of three with a booming mail order quilt shop—I was stretched thin. Quilter friends invited me to go with them to Baltimore. The quilts were big, bright, and powerful. I came to stand transfixed before the last quilt. It had a red wheel of hearts at its center. I felt drawn to that block as though it were speaking to me, but in a tongue I couldn't quite understand. Unaccountably, tears welled in my eyes. I felt as though I were looking into the soul of the woman who had made it. Fingers long stilled, those Album makers touched and transformed me. I could not wait to get home to make their patterns.

When I started my research, odd things jumped out at me. Acorns stitched into cornucopias of fruit; baskets of flowers; and wreaths of oak leaves. Why acorns? I wondered. A Victorian book, *The Language of Flowers*, told me that acorns symbolized longevity, and oak leaves meant strength against adversity. What happy wishes to stitch into a quilt! That pattern series grew into a book—24 patterns illustrating a dictionary of symbols. I took a bank loan the size of a college tuition and self-published this book.

At 1983's Quilt Market, I carried an armful of these books, hot off the press, to three book distributors. Then I sat down for a lecture called "Publish . . .. or Be Published?" The speaker held up my book! "What is this about?" she asked. "*Spoken Without a Word.*" That title surely doesn't tell us! This book will never sell," she predicted. "It is the wrong size. It won't fit on people's shelves. It won't fit in distributors' boxes. And look, there's no color. It costs $12.95; people will never pay $12.95 for no color!" There goes that tuition, I thought.

But from that book, something grew. Invitations to teach started arriving. As an old history teacher who couldn't control seventh graders, that book was my ticket to paradise—teaching appliqué to grown-up women. It began a multi-book, multi-decade journey.

Fascinated by the Baltimores, I dug up more about symbols and the Album era. Picture, for example, an appliqué of two hearts, overlapped and pierced by an arrow. You and I might think "romance"! But in the library I found an old handbook, *The Oddfellows' Monitor and Guide*, and quite a different meaning. "Two hearts linked by an arrow," it said, symbolize one Brother's willingness to go to the aid—to give his life if necessary—for another brother. Turns out the album quilt era coincided with the Mexican-American War. Baltimore sent a battalion of her sons to fight for the Texan Americans' freedom [to become the 28th state] and stitched that story into her quilts.

I found that those same symbols stitched onto Victorian quilts—doves, laurel wreaths, hands, lilies, urns, and roses—are also carved into Victorian tombstones. This is important. It tells us that this use of symbols was "dead serious"!

Some years ago, a prehistoric man, "Otzi," was found frozen in Switzerland. The anthropologist sculpting his likeness noted that when you work so closely with something old, and human, you cannot help but feel a spiritual connectedness to it. As I worked on the old quilts, that happened to me. It is the mystery of our connectedness to others. Not literally, in the sense of held hands or shared conversations, but spiritually, in a shared understanding of our very humanness, of our brief time here on this earth.

What one gift from the Old Albums might we single out? Above and beyond all the fascination and fancywork, I appreciate the witness they bear to the SPIRIT in which a person plays the hand she's dealt. The Album makers' troubles were surely no less than our own, yet they left us such a gift of beauty! In *The Pursuit of Excellence*, Charles Murray writes, "Ask yourself: What sculpture, novel, or painting . . . produced *since* 1950 will *still* be considered important 200 years from now?"

His theory is that great accomplishment in the arts has been fostered by transcendent goals like Truth and Goodness. "Without

these high goals," he suggests, "art can rise to the highest rungs of craft, captivating entertainments can be produced. But in the same way that a goldsmith needs gold, a culture needs a coherent sense of the transcendent to foster great accomplishment."

This is intriguing, for some say we live in a secular age. Yet who cannot but look around this convention center hung with glorious quilts and ask, will the future not find at least some of this work worth labeling "Classic"? And does a search for the transcendent have something to do with it?

Let's listen to some brief answers, inscribed on the old Albums. Judge whether they convey a Reach for the Good, the True, and the Beautiful.

- "May you, my child, in Virtue's path proceed. /Her ways are pleasant and to Heaven lead. /Then when you leave this tenement of clay/ Angels shall guide you to the realm of day."

OR,

- To General Taylor of the Rio Grande, From your Rough and Ready. E Pluribus Unum.

And another message,

- "Let all inspired with Godly mirth/ Sing solemn hymns of Praise." — inscribed "March, 1844"

The most common inscription is some version of "*Remember* me:"

- "Should I be parted far from thee/Look at this and think of me."

And on another quilt, a reply:

- "I'll remember dear Angie, whatever betide/ I'll remember you ALWAYS/ Tho waters . . . divide."

What might make a quilt a "Classic"? As Murray writes: "In some cases, it is not the clarity of their understanding, but the persistence of the seeking that enables people to achieve great things. The enduring image of human accomplishments is not what the

"Stitching Baltimore Album blocks is a gift of my heart, a shared understanding, a sense of feeling together and being connected though friendships and our common love of a needle."

—Sandra Rochon

giants did, but how they did it. Most, even those who fit the image of the genius, resembled the craftsman at his bench, struggling to get things right, agonizing over mistakes, and doing work over again, with a vision of perfection insistently pulling them onward."

We've read some of the Old Ones' messages. What message will our own quilts leave to the future? Several years ago, a fellow quilt teacher gave white buttons in class that read, "No Whining." One sees no whining on the Old Albums, nor on the New. I've never heard whining in an Album class. We know many among us, perhaps all of us, have had sorrows and loss, bitter disappointments of the most personal kind. Yet a quilt class is a happy place, full of easy laughter. All the quilters I have known have been quietly courageous. They've met life with grace. The Old Albums' message is faith, hope, and love; many of our quilts echo that message. Surely our perserverance must also shine through.

People argue that we are a secular culture, a culture with no common transcendent purpose—that increasingly, we may not even have a common culture. I'm not sure this is true. For a time after 9/11, we discovered a lot of unity. Even before 9/11, today's quilters protected their unity. Have you noticed that at a quilt conference, no one ever asks, "What kind of work do you do?" They know what you do that's important: You Quilt. Without giving it much thought, quilters stitch clear of dissension. It is as though we have an unwritten rule: to concentrate on the things that unite us and avoid things that might divide us. I've noticed religion and politics, for example, just never *come up* in my classes, even around election time.

I love the Quilt Guild ritual of Show and Tell most of all for what it says about quilters. As we show a quilt—for a brief moment—the audience tries to see the world as we do, and supports us with a round of applause.

Drawing to a close, I was a little girl, long ago, a little girl who loved making things. I grew up to find Paradise teaching appliqué to grown women. I am overwhelmingly honored and touched by the Silver Star because it seems to put a comforting arm around me for . . . well, for being myself. I am all the less lonely for knowing this gift, this esoteric quilt style I love and learned about; is a gift now widely shared. I became a quiltmaker, then an appliquér, and I think appliqué makes beautiful quilts. But I believe doing appliqué also beautifies our souls.

The old quilts bear witness to wisdom. They give us comfort and courage in our time of need. They give us such joy! This art, the old *and* the new, helps explain us to ourselves, ties past to present—and us to the future. Both the old ones and the new ones bear witness to lives that accept and rejoice in the day which the Lord has made.

We're told we're spoiled here in this land of milk and honey. But I've heard no whining in our classes; I've seen none on the Albums. All I've heard is needles singing a joyful chorus. The voices in our Albums are aunts and mothers, daughters and sisters, grandmothers and wives. They speak their love through their quilts. They will continue to speak when the hand that made them is stilled. In closing, here's just one contemporary Album inscription, to speak for us all. It's from a quilt in the show called:

A Tisket-a-Tasket
I'm growing old but I still try to create,
*   with tiny scraps of fabric,*
*   brightly colored, — like jewels,*
*   to take the form of the flowers and leaves*
I've always loved on my journey through life.
I dream on, it seems, to live.
Dreams are much akin to prayers,
*   so my lips, from time to time, move silently,*
*   as my fingers stitch*
*   tiny pieces of cloth into these floral*
*   arrangements*
to fill the baskets that I dare to believe /
*   you may enjoy seeing.*
And perhaps, see a bit of me /
*   as your eyes travel from basket to basket.*
Made by Marjorie Mahoney, Age 80

And the gift you and I bequeath to the future? A happy thought: If we give a fraction of the joy to people yet unborn that the old quilts have given us, we will have done good in this world.

Picture a woman 150 years from now, stitching quietly on a quilt inspired by an Old One, inscribed "November, 2003." Smiling to herself, she's thinking a thank you for our gift—our Old Quilt. Our own quilt will surely answer for us, "You're most welcome. It was our pleasure."

JANET GUNN SEWELL

"When life gets hectic, stitching allows me the time reflect on my life—blessings, challenges, family. As I look at the quilts I've made, so many memories come back to me of things that might otherwise be forgotten. They are a story to me, an unexpected gift."
—Cheri Leffler

JANET ZEHR ESCH

"By recreating the beautiful needlework that was lovingly, meticulously crafted by those women of Baltimore, who were striving for beauty while conveying unspoken meanings, we connect to their creative process while giving our spark of consciousness a tangible witness for our children to appreciate."

—Kathryn Bernstein

SWAW 2014's Needleartists

Bette Florette Leonard Augustine

Bette's grandmother and mother both instilled in her a love of needle and thread. Formerly a legal secretary and librarian, Bette recently retired from her position as Administrator for TESAA. She lives in California, happily married with 2 children and 2 beautiful granddaughters.

Mary Kiefer Beals

Mary has always been an avid needle worker. After raising her children, she moved to California and taught school for 26 years. Now retired, she has learned to quilt: needleturn appliqué, hand and machine piecing and quilting. Quilting is her form of relaxation!

Linda Bear

Linda now teaches stitching skills and techniques of yesteryear, as well as designing quilts reminiscent of the 1800s. She researches a quilt's style and blends it with her "Australian tilt" to create something unique, ready to reveal a story.

Kathryn Bernstein

Kathryn lives in LA with her husband and is the proud stepmother of 4 lovely children. She comes from a quilting family, who instilled in her a love and appreciation of the art. Kathryn loves history and collects vintage textiles, which she hopes to use in her quilts someday.

Mary Ann (Carvelho) Bloom

Retired after 38 years of teaching, Mary Ann enjoys scrapbooking, gardening, and quilting—especially BAQ appliqué. Mary Ann has been married for 38 years and is the mother of 2 sons and 2 grandchildren. She lives in California.

Susan Bradshaw

When Susan first tried quilting 15 years ago, she knew she had found her life's vocation. Susan enjoys all quilting, but a needleturn appliqué class from Rita Verroca has sent her on a hand-quilting adventure. Susan lives in West Hills, CA.

Anne Carter

Anne is a devoted wife, a mother of 2 wonderful daughters, a fraternal twin, and a CPA. She began as a self-taught quilter and subsequently attended one of Elly's excellent classes, along with some other talented teachers. Anne lives in Rochester, NH.

Nadine Cassady

Nadine's mother and grandmother inspired her to make quilts. In her family's business, she made spacecraft parts for Mars; she has also made blocks from 1850 Album Quilts. Both are important to her, as are her husband, 2 daughters, 3 grandchildren, and 2 great-grandchildren.

"Appliqué and all it entails has never been a hobby for me, but rather a calling which I know beckons softly to others who are in search of their artistic voice."

—Bette F. Augustine

Nancy Chesney-Smith

Nancy and her husband live in Southern CA, where they raised their daughters. When she holds a quilt that her great-grandmother and great-aunt made together, she remembers them with love. To Nancy, a signed block is a true gift of being remembered.

Evelyn Crovo-Hall

Her expert seamstress mother taught Evelyn to stitch, and they made their first quilt together. After retiring from teaching, Evelyn attended TESAA yearly. Combining her two passions, teaching and quilting, she was honored to be part of TESAA faculty.

Barbara Dahl

Barbara has been sewing since she was 10, following her mother and grandmother, both skilled needlewomen. Barbara finds hand sewing relaxing, and the creativity of "painting" with fabric feeds her soul. She has recently moved from California to Hawaii.

Joan Dorsay

Joan has been quilting for more than 30 years and has won many awards for her quilts, both in Canada and the US. Her passion is for hand appliqué and quilting. Since her 2007 retirement, she is completing her third Baltimore Album Quilt. Joan lives in Ottawa, Canada.

Katherine Scott Hudgins Dunigan

Kathy began quilting in 1987 and discovered appliqué in 1993, in a Baltimore Album class, taught from a book by "our Elly." She has taught in the U.S. and Canada. She and her husband live in Rockwell, Texas, and celebrate three beautiful children.

Janet Zehr Esch

After retiring from teaching in 2003, Janet joined the Baltimore Appliqué Society in Maryland and was thrust into the rich history of these beautiful quilts. She has completed two Baltimore Album quilts, one honoring her daughter and one honoring her family of origin.

Ellen Heck

About 20 years ago, Ellen discovered quilts, especially the beautiful Baltimore Albums. She enjoys all aspects of quilting, especially appliqué. Ellen has made several quilts, won awards, exhibited in Europe and Japan, and taught at TESAA. She lives in California.

Gena Holland

When Gena first saw *SWAW* in 1983, she knew that one day she had to make a Baltimore Album quilt. A former clinical social worker, Gena now focuses totally on her passion for appliqué. She is thankful that her dear husband supports and encourages her addiction.

Delia P. Kane

Delia was born in Italy and came to the United States in 1956. Upon retirement from her career in law enforcement in New Jersey, she wanted an "American" hobby and chose quiltmaking. A self-taught quilter, Delia now teaches appliqué at a local quilt shop.

Carolyn Goff Kimble

Carolyn has lived in Big Point, MS, all her life. She enjoys sharing time with her family and her quilting hobby. After many years of quilting, she is finding that embroidery, appliqué, and hand quilting are her very favorites.

GENA HOLLAND

"It is an absolute joy being part of a sisterhood passing the love of these wonderful quilts on to future generations."

—Gena Holland

Jessica LaMar

Jessica saw her first quilt in about 1948 at her grandmother's house when a neighbor came to show off her work with a glorious appliquéd floral wreath and border. Jessica's yearning for that quilt has taken her on a lifelong journey of learning, stitching, and collecting.

Marcie Lane

Her grandmother started Marcie's stitching journey when she was 4, teaching her embroidery. Hand appliqué is now her passion. When she first saw a Baltimore Album, she knew she wanted to make one. Marcie has won awards for her work and teaches at a local quilt shop.

Cheri Leffler

The needle talents of her great-grandmother and mother fascinated Cheri. She is mostly self-taught but has taken appliqué classes from Elly. Cheri enjoys this art form and smiles when thinking of her work being held and handed down through future generations.

Fiona Lindsay

Fiona is a third generation quiltmaker, rare in her native Australia. Her aim is for her work to be a celebration of creativity and color, and hand appliqué is her preferred method of expression. Fiona is married and has two adult children.

Melissa Simross

Melissa has been quilting for 17 years and has found her true passion: Baltimore Album quilts. She first attended TESAA in 2006 and started her first Baltimore Album, designing several blocks based on her life and embellishing blocks from Elly's books.

MELISSA SIMROSS

"Baltimore Album stitching seems to give me a calm I can't really explain. Along with the calm resulting from the stitching, I get a feeling of contentment knowing someone, a long time from now, is going to look at my stitching, think of me, and know that I existed."

—Marcie Lane

Rosalynn McKown

At age 49, Rosalynn found herself hooked on Baltimore Album quilting in a class with Mimi Dietrich in Baltimore. She moved to Florida, joined an appliqué guild, and took some classes with Elly. Rosalynn has completed four album quilts and started her next project.

Karen Moraal

Karen became enamored with Baltimore Album Quilts when Elly's *Baltimore Elegance* was published. Karen is a single mother of 2 wonderful boys and has a stressful, demanding job. Quilting is her passion and keeps her centered. Stitching soothes her soul.

Karen Pessia

Karen has been a quiltmaker for nearly 30 years. Her true love, appliqué, has put her on an incredible, creative, and passionate journey, bringing her great teachers and wonderful friendships. Karen now teaches others about Baltimore Album Quilts and needleturn appliqué.

Sandra Reynolds

Sandy started quilting in the late 1970's, inspired by her mother. Appliqué is her passion and meditation. Sandy's "My Tree of Life Quilt" is her act of love for her family—her amazing parents and sister, and her beloved husband, children, and grandchildren.

Sandra Rochon

The needle skills and talents of her Mom, Grandma, and Great-grandmother inspired Sandra as a needleartist. She began exploring the world of appliqué in the early 1990's. Sandra currently resides in Calgary, Alberta with her loving and supportive husband.

Margaret Russell

Margaret has always loved textiles, but as a mother, stockbroker, teacher and administrator, she was too busy to pursue her interest. After retiring, she took an appliqué class and her interest became obsession, finding something meditative in the rhythm of stitching.

Janet Gunn Sewell

After raising 2 daughters, Janet found some quilt blocks her grandmother had not assembled and learned to quilt. She took a Baltimore appliqué class and loves how each block preserves family history and the history of our country. Janet lives in Rapid City, SD.

Jeanne Sullivan

Jeanne has always loved being creative with needle and thread. A retired principal, she spends nearly every waking hour immersed in fabric and fiber. Author of *Simply Successful Appliqué,* Jeanne teaches and is proud to include TESAA on her national teaching schedule.

Ardeth (Ardie) Sveadas

Ardie first learned embroidery from her grandmothers. Her first quilt was a baby quilt for her son in 1962, and she became addicted. Ardie lives in Michigan with her husband. She has grown children and six grandchildren—all warmed by one of her quilts.

Madeline Swope

When she was young, Madeline sewed clothing, for herself and her children. When she retired from a hospital financial office, Madeline saw some quilts a friend had made, and she got hooked. Madeline lives in California.

Rosalind Wood Thébaud

Rosalind grew up in a Baltimore suburb and saw Baltimore album quilts at an early age, fascinated with the workmanship. She's been on her appliqué journey for 40 years, attempting to 'master' the technique and beauty of BAQs. Rosalind lives in California.

Yolanda (Yoly) Tovar

As a child, Yoly learned embroidery, from which her love of creating beautiful precise stitching began. Her first encounter with a Baltimore Album Quilt was in the 80s in a class with Elly. This was when her two loves merged—embroidery and appliqué.

Mary K. Tozer

Mary has been quilting for over 20 years. Formerly a geologist, she now works for a major agricultural company. The two constant obsessions in her life are her family and her obsession with all things connected to quilting and fiber. Mary lives in Rogers, Minnesota.

Rita Verroca

Born and raised in Germany, Rita fell in love with quilts 30 years ago. She has made many quilts, and she most treasures hand quilting, which breathes a soul into her quilts. Living in LA, Rita is a passionate teacher and enjoys sharing her knowledge with her students.

Edie Zakem

Edie was smitten by Baltimore Album quilts at the time *Spoken Without a Word* was published, both by the book and the sentiment of the title. She has been happily chasing that dream ever since. Edie lives in beautiful Prince Edward Island on Canada's east coast.

"In an age when fashions and trends come and go at an ever quickening pace and life often feels like a treadmill set at a too-fast speed, needlework is a peaceful oasis where work stays done and one just might create beauty that can last a century or more."

—Margaret Russell

"The BAQ is still a way for a woman to tell her story; a means for her to leave a legacy for her children and generations to follow. When doing hand piecing or hand appliqué, each stitch becomes a prayer, a time of reflection. There is a beauty in the quietness of creating a BAQ."

—Rosalind Wood Thébaud

Epilogue

MISS CHASE would inform her friends and customers that she has on hand some MUSLINS, of superior quality, which were exhibited at the Mechanics' Fair, in this city, a few weeks ago; colored Cambrics 4 and 6 cts per yd; fine Calico Prints, fast colors, 6¼; Ginghams 12½; Silk Rouches 6¼ cts; Linen Hdkfs 6¼; ladies' French Kid GLOVES 31¼; Comforts 8 cts; Pins 3 cts a paper; articles suitable for funeral occasions, such as Flannels, Satins, Crapes, Cambrics, &c. A few ALBUM SQUARES, for quilts, very handsome; steel Bead RETICULES, new style.

MISS CHASE is prepared to attend to all kinds of plain and fancy MILLINERY. Bleaching and Pressing done in the neatest style, at her STORE, j20-swtf31* corner of Eutaw and Biddle sts.

Clues in the Classifieds . . . a taste of things to come.

"*In the years between 1846 and 1852, there emerged in Baltimore a group of quilts that comprise an exceptional and brilliant artistic entity, with distinctive features that set them apart from other quilts of the same period.*"

—Dena Katzenberg, *Baltimore Album Quilts*

Entrepreneurial and driven, the Ladies of Baltimore would seem by the evidence to have applied Industry's assembly line principles by having cutters and basters for appliqué motif units in quilt production: interchangeable parts for certain blocks and undulating swag or vine borders. Witnesses confirming this hypothesis accumulate. One is generously shared by Album scholar Ronda McAllen, with her 'find' in the ads pictured above. Today's Album-makers came to recognize in Baltimore's 'High-Style,' its defining Principles and Elements of Design. Those antebellum quilts *mapped these out* so clearly, that we moderns, following those antebellum Album maps, have copied, innovated, and masterfully created echoes of that period-style art. Some contemporary artists, in homage to the style, have sought to reproduce the look; others have taken it to soar exuberantly, far 'beyond Baltimore.'

Circa 1846–1852, Albums came to bloom, sophisticated Baltimore was bus-tling—an international port, a manufacturing, commercial, cultural, philanthropic, and political hub. She was an *arts*-centered city. MICA's Historical Timeline shows that Fine Arts and Drawing classes had been open to women at Baltimore's Maryland Institute for the Promotion of the Mechanic Arts since 1826. Might these factors help explain what drove the Ladies of Baltimore to become a veritable *hive* of quiltmaking industry? Good humored and hardworking, did they 'spoof' *themselves*— as two notable Album inscriptions suggest? One such "humorous imitation" adorns a famous High-Style Album bordered by a lushly undulating floral wreath—its open ends make it a symbolic "*crown*" (of laurel for '*superior merit*' and of roses, '*victory*'). Firmly ensconced on a pediment of posies sits a sturdy *beehive*, symbol of *Unity* and *Strength in Community*. Around it, ink-inscribed *bees* (conveying the traits 'zealous and industrious') swarm most busily. Embellishment's flourish, yes. But a sig-

nature perhaps? Bees personifying Baltimore's diligent Ladies?

What might have been their motivation? One senses that it was more than simple entrepreneurialism. Capitalism and commerce, yes, but message-bearing and principled, duty-bound and exhilarated—'Doing well,' as the saying goes, 'by doing good.' Published reports confirm that these women's artwork drew public acclaim—in their hometown, in beloved "Baltie"—in their own time. With the clues in the classifieds, above, we have a taste of the story promised in this book's sequel—even as *SWAW2014* here draws to a close.

"On January 20, 1849, a small advertisement appeared on page 2 in *The Sun* Newspaper of Baltimore," Ronda McAllen, who discovered these ads, writes:

"Are these the professionally designed and basted squares which reappear in the Album quilts during this period? The following year at the 1849 Mechanics' Fair, Mary Chase deposited several "fancy patchwork quilts," one of which won her first prize in the needlework category. Could this fancy patchwork quilt have been made from the blocks she advertised in January and considered part of the album quilt craze? Who is Miss Chase at the corner of Eutaw and Biddle streets? The 1848–49 Matchett's city directories list a Miss

Mary Chase, fancy dry goods and milliner, sw corner Eutaw and Biddle streets. The 1850 U.S. Census places Mary Chase in Ward 20 living with the Toft family and owns real estate valued at $1,000."

*"Late in the Album quilt period, on November 20, 1858, another advertisement appeared in Baltimore's Sun Newspaper for the December issue of the "**Illustrated Mirror of Fashion and Lady's Newspaper.**" The contents for the December issue contain a "**Design for Album Patchwork.**" These advertisements, along with Hannah Trimble's diary entries, appear to suggest the existence of a 'professional' group of needle artists who designed and produced basted blocks to sell, possibly through fancy dry goods or millinery stores, many of which were owned by Baltimore women. Further research may well piece together the patchwork of this most intriguing mystery."*

Most of Old Baltimore's Albums seem to have been stitched "communally," in circles that shared faith and family, patriotism, heroes, and politics. Some makers, we are led to believe, hung their quilts in the large first-floor windows of that era's Old Town Baltimore homes, often 'signalling' commercial space—homes perhaps, of milliners, dressmakers, and other fabric arts professionals.[1] Might some of the quilts

Stitching these complicated and time-consuming blocks has forced me to discipline myself to take time out from a busy day and spend it on reflection and on creating beautiful things. I now 'stop and smell the roses.'"
—Delia P. Kane

1 Years ago, Ronda McAllen, in conversation, described political iconography in the quilts, and suggested that quilts may have been hung in the commerce-inviting Old Town Windows. (Debbie Cooney pictures just such a windowed-house in her Samuel Williams Quilt article on www.baltimoreapplique.com/williams.) Iconography in the Samuel Williams quilt is a chapter in *Spoken Without a Word Volume II—Baltimore's Antebellum Album Quilts, History and Hypotheses.* While this Epilogue is written in a manner more conversational than scholarly, specific source citation follows this subject in *Volume II.*

thus hung, on some occasions, have been electioneering? Though unenfranchised, the women were avid supporters of their political favorites and by instantly recognized symbols, appliquéd them boldly into their art. Were these quilts a must-see for ladies and gentlemen out on a fine day's walk around Old Town Baltimore? Its city's *Sun* newspaper reflects strong interest in *the ladies'* work and urges them to bring it for exhibition to the 1848 grand opening of the Maryland Institute Fair. Like Ronda's multiple professionals involved in selling prefabricated blocks, here is a fascinating history worth further exploration.

Earlier, we considered Charles Murray's postulate that for art to be meaningful, enduring, it must have something of the transcendent about it, some reach for the 'Good, True, and Beautiful.' His insight cannot be original, but it is good for the human soul to reconsider it periodically. I recently came across a variant echoed in an Album Era quote from the Reverend J. A. Seiss, Pastor of the Lombard Street Lutheran Church in Baltimore City, Maryland. Seiss, a prominent religious speaker, said the following at an 1850s Maryland Institute Women's Division graduation address:

> *"Beauty is an element of good, a joyous symbol of the Divine. A genuine perception of it is the highest degree of education, and the ultimate polish of man. . . . Just as we teach people, then, to detect, appreciate and produce the beautiful, we contribute to swell the sum of human virtue and felicity, and help to make them happier, better and more useful."*[2]

The Maryland Institute for the Promotion of the Mechanic Arts, and the work of professional artists and seamstresses in Baltimore's antique Beauties, are central to Old Baltimore's Album story.[3] But the drive which leads to masterpiece 'Baltimores' today may well arise from the same source that Reverend Seiss describes in his address, asserting that all human accomplishment, which might be called 'civilization,' is neither an accident, nor purely a gift from God, but rather the product of human striving for good, truth, and beauty, which is central to the "mysterious arrangement of Providence." *Self-improvement*—that ubiquitous phrase for principled, virtuous striving—was the American attitude from the time John Winthrop first preached uprightness to the Pilgrims arriving at the *Plymouth Plantacion*, to Album Era and into the 20th century.

Might all this be why stitching old Baltimore's path gives so many of us such joy? This book's Introduction asked, gentle reader, if we moderns might share a specific goal with Baltimore's Antebellum

> *"I can pick up a block, thread my needle with a fine piece of silk thread, and proceed to lose myself completely in the peaceful stitching of my block—all cares disappear, and I am filled with comfort and peace in mind, body, and soul."*
>
> —Sandra Reynolds

2 Joseph Augustus Seiss, *The Arts Of Design* (Baltimore: J. Murphy & Co., 1857), 8.

3 The author's forthcoming books and their CreateSpace eStore links will be on www.AppliqueWithElly.com at the time of publication. In the works are *Spoken Without a Word, Volume II, Baltimore's Antebellum Album Quilts, History and Hypotheses*, followed by *Beatific Baltimore Album Quilts, Patterns and Processes*, with expertise shared by contemporary artists. These future books, as published, will be available on www.amazon.com.

"Numsen Family Lyre" by Elly Sienkiewicz, who inscribed this antique pattern with a banner in memory of her father.

"Love and Honor" by Maryann McFee, who reproduced this classic block to commemorate her husband. Its Lyre symbolizes "All music in honor of God."

Album artists. That goal is surely Beauty, is it not? They and we seek to create—guided by Beauty's transcendence. Perhaps, you, too, have found faith, and hope, and love thereby.

Our contemporary needle-sisters' work is this book's treasure trove, each speaking from her heart. How blessed are we, to have been born into this turn of the century Album Revival! From those antebellum classics, we have learned so much—history, for example. But more intimately, those Albums offer us witness to their own deep faith and love of country. Keeping their company—and yours—gives me courage in this troubled world. Family and teaching 'the Albums' centered my young and middle years. Now retired from traveling to teach, I'm looking forward to finishing several books well underway—opening more of the time allotted us on this good Earth to the blessings of family. Beyond old friends and family, my greatest joy has been to come to know you with whom I have had the privilege to share the Albums. You have been to me a wellspring of faith, hope, and love. Even as I write this, you make my heart smile.

—Elly Sienkiewicz
Washington, DC May 28, 2014

"Crown of Laurel with Rose" by Elly Sienkiewicz for her deceased father. Design and inscription from a marble monument in First Presbyterian Church graveyard, Kings Highway, Lewes, DE. The inscription reads:
DEAREST FATHER, YOU HAVE LEFT US
HERE THY LOSS WE DEEPLY FEEL
BUT TIS GOD THAT HATH BEREFT US
HE SHALL ALL OUR SORROWS HEAL.
—Mid-19th Century Tombstone

Budded on Earth to Bloom in Heaven

A WHITE ROSEBUD (YOUTH, purity, innocence) on Baltimore-era gravestones is one of several symbols for a dear child dying young. One comes, sometimes, upon the rosebud epitaph in graveyards where old roses bloom. That tragedy is timeless: a single rosebud on a time-worn marker; on another, a marble rosebud—just one of five carved on a bush, cut and floating, free. How does one commemorate kin killed by evil? Through symbols of immortal love.

When their mother, Katherine Sydnor, died in the Lord's good time, she had recently made the block pictured on her monument for Appliqué by the Bay's quilt, pictured in *Elly Sienkiewicz's Beloved Baltimore Albums* and hung at Houston's "Baltimore's Daughters" exhibition. Katherine was a friend to all, a prolific and talented quiltmaker. Her daughters, Bonnie Esterly and Connie Allen, designed her commemorative, engraving it with this apt antique needlework inscription: *"I pray that risen from the dead, I may in glory stand. A crown perhaps upon my head, but a needle in my hand."* With a flower 'for the beauty and brevity of life,' and a bird symbolizing 'life of the soul,' the inscription at the stone's base speaks eloquently: *"Cherished Memories Stitched in our Hearts Forever."* Kinsale Cemetery, Virginia.

Relic of the Oklahoma bombing, April 19, 1995, this bud metaphor from our Victorian past ties one's soul to the future. A carved epitaph, it seeks solace over horror in the hard, gentle beauty of faithful acceptance. Rose Hill Cemetery, Oklahoma.

Afterword

Remembering: The Elly Sienkiewicz Appliqué Academy 1995 – 2014

"Nothing lasts, like a happy memory."

Dear Friends,

Happy Spring! Miss Tesaa, The Elly Sienkiewicz Appliqué Academy, finished its 19th year this February. We were overjoyed that so many friends could come—the new, the familiar, and all filled with gratitude. We were all so excited! Williamsburg's James River-edge resort site was new to Tesaa and so beautiful. The Academicians were superb, the faculty excellent, the food delicious, the entertainment so fine, the conference impeccably run and elegantly hostessed by staff and volunteers.

Since this time together was perfect—and fate at conference end determined that it cannot be repeated—Appliqué Academy 2014 became Miss Tesaa's last. The perfect ending at the perfect place! Of course closing was bittersweet for you and for us, and you are rightly curious. Miss Tesaa has been owned by Elly, and administered, these past 16 of its 19 years, by Bette. An especially precious few have attended since the beginning to be joined by so many wonderful others.

At February Academy's end, her Administrator, Bette, retired, having just learned of her sister's critical need for care. We, all pictured nearby, talked. Miss Tesaa's wonderful hostess team admitted the blessing of years was nudging them past her heavy behind-the-scenes work. Then, too, Elly needed to shed Tesaa and teaching to bring first *Spoken Without a Word, 30th Anniversary Edition* to press and to fulfill other commitments. We all loved our jobs and *You*, "The Academicians", our friends.

Probably for you as well as for us, Miss Tesaa had become a wellspring of warmth in this vast universe we call home. Her focused studies gave us a common bond. Her joy, and now such happy memories of you uplift us. You had brought TESAA to life. Oh, the Albums! Forthrightly, Album sisters of long ago inscribed the plea, *"Remember me."* Miss Tesaa's mission was *Art and Friendship*. You gave us both. We will always Remember Thee.

In fond friendship,
Elly, Bette, and Tesaa Hostesses, too.

Post Script: This letter announced that 'TESAA,' the much-loved annual appliqué school gathering was officially closed. First of the international conferences devoted to Baltimore and appliqué's art, it had begun in Annapolis, Maryland, moved to Lewes, Delaware, and thence to Williamsburg, Virginia, over the course of two decades. Each setting, like the quilts this art school lauded, was historic—and beautiful. A certain portion of its more than 200 "Academicians" and faculty stayed the same, while others changed. We all came to study the Baltimores, appliqué, and what the nineteenth century called, "The Ornamental Arts." This recent ending has turned out to be a beginning. For within this year, three new conferences studying these ornamental arts have opened around the country. What more propitious bell could possibly have rung for us, we who join together to commemorate the Baltimore Album Revival?

"Baltimore Album Quilts. I love them. I just love them. I can't say why. Is it because the detail in some is exquisite while the quirkiness in others simply charming? Perhaps it's the sheer scale of dedication required to produce a quilt of such beauty. Possibly. Or is it simply that they are just beautiful, beautiful works of art. All I know is that I just can't help myself. I love them."

—Fiona Lindsay,
Melbourne, Australia

And are we not so blessed? "Love" is a word of many hues. Its rainbow seems to have permeated Baltimore's classes where, though strangers, we came as friends. And so with Miss Tesaa. Dear Academicians, Volunteers, Bette and Staff, Faculty, and never-met "List Visit friends," it is my privilege to know and love you—for even we who had no conversation, know that where we gathered, we formed a 'sisterhood.' What lasting comfort your company in community will always give me. We've been borne upon a wonderful, wonderful journey together!

—Elly S.

Left to right, top row: **Kathy Breidenstein, Jan Vaine, Doris Seeley**
Center row: **Kara Mason, Jo Cridge**
Bottom row: **Teri Young, Bette Augustine, Diana Phillips,** and **Elly**
Not pictured: **Megan Sutton**

Deep in the Territory

By Margaret Fleischer Kaufman

Even the trees are different here,
Don't look right, bend toward the river in a foreign way
Like women washing laundry over stones.

Three years since we saw you,
Stopped in this prairie town so far
From home, deep in the Territory.
Still it startles me when Indian women appear –
I never hear them –
They are suddenly quietly there
Leaning into the shade of the house
Against the Kansas glare.

I'm used to calling solitude my friend,
George travelling so far from farm to farm
But it slips through my fingers when the women come.
I confess myself glad to greet them
Though it troubles me the way they walk right in,
As if our house were landscape only.

I can tell they don't admire my tea.
What draws them is the album quilt.
They never take their silent leave
Without standing at our bed, touching it.
They turn it all around, tug the binding.
I stand there watching much like
Women with babies when strangers
Pinch their cheeks, nervous
Yet proud like that, fearful
In the odd, cold way that fear takes hold
When there's no common tongue.

How can I sign "friend" to them,
Explain that Edith stitched those wreaths,
Evaline, the goose tracks pointing out?
As if it were yesterday
I see us working at the frame
In the church hall Wednesday nights.
Though it puzzles them, I chant your names
To the Indian women: "Edith," I whisper,
"Evaline, Mary Lou."

Acknowledgements

UNLIKE *Spoken Without a Word, 1983 (SWAW1983)* **Spoken Without a Word, 30th Anniversary Edition** *(SWAW2014)* would have been inconceivable but for quiltmaking's cherished tradition of sharing. Some thirty years ago, relatively few were devoted to the art of appliqué. Pieced quilts reigned. None back then could have envisioned the revivalist outpouring yet to come. Surely none foresaw the heights of beauty to which appliqué would again aspire—once having been exposed by the Baltimore Album Revival and antebellum Album Quilts: "Classics that set a standard for all time."

Beyond words, this *Baltimore Album Revival Commemorative Edition* is beholden to contributing needleartists whose work fills her pages with stitched glory. Regrettably, space restraints have precluded some needleartists' works, photographs, written words. My gratitude remains. Thank you one and all. Marcel Proust spoke for us as we prepared this edition, "Let us be grateful to people who make us happy, for they are the charming gardeners who make our souls blossom."

CUSTOMIZED CONTRIBUTIONS TO THIS COMMEMORATIVE EDITION:

- Margaret Fleischer Kaufman, poetess and college classmate. Though not a quilter, she read my books' historic notes and unpublished Numsen family records, then mailed me such a gift! For "future Baltimore books": four lyrical poems by her hand. Two that appeared in *Baltimore Beauties and Beyond, Volume II* are within, for they address the origins and allure of Baltimore's Old Albums. The remaining poems concern some of the mystery that still clings to this quiltstyle. They will be in this book's sequel on its "History and Hypotheses."

- Rita Verroca designed an all *SWAW-patterned* quilt for our Quilt Gallery, then with these gathered friends—Mary

ANN NASH

Beals, Kathryn Bernstein, Susan Bradshaw, Nadine Cassady, Nancy Chesney-Smith, Barbara Dahl, Mary Fischel, Ellen Heck, Jessica LaMar, Margaret Russel, Ann Rust, Madeline Swope, and Ros Thébaud—stitched the blocks exquisitely to life.

- Sandy Reynolds gave her charming "Tree of Life Quilt" pattern's first publication rights to this Edition (p. 32).

- Dawn Licker here shares her original wall quilt pattern designed for the "Elly Sienkiewicz for Robert Kaufman *Spoken Without a Word*" designer fabric line.

- Bette Augustine, formerly The Elly Sienkiewicz Applique Academy®'s Administrator, stitched this book's cover block. Its wondrously interpreted solo sings praise and gratitude for antebellum appliqué's gifts of heart and hand.

Those most closely involved with this new book are:

- Teri Young, my Administrative Assistant of many hats, companion-chaplain; editor-friend; all that and Helmsman, too;

- Sue Hartman, book designer—her vision transcends; her ability to translate it into print, remarkable; getting to know her, a joy; (my gratitude as well to Ed Hartman: his high-tech photographic skills, artistry, and supportive input surely have enhanced this book's beauty www.suettcommunications.com);

- Mary Fox Skelton with great good cheer and her third hand, manages www.AppliqueWithElly.com, my book and DVD fulfillment site;

- Stan Sienkiewicz, beloved helpmeet, is the wondrous enabler to his authoress Baltimore bride.

My heart-felt Thank you, Each and All.

Elly Sienkiewicz

Washington, DC 5.18.14

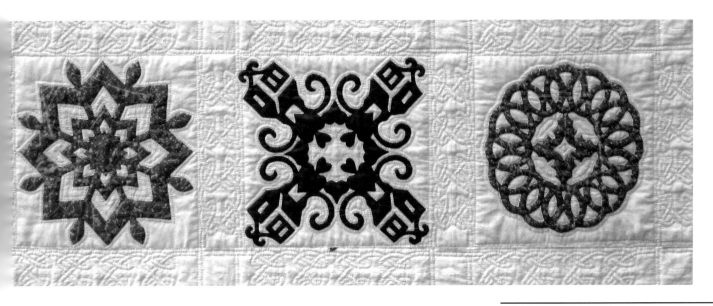

About the Author

ELLY SIENKIEWICZ, of Washington D.C.

ELLY LOVES HER FAMILY, country, and quilt-art—in that order. As a young mother, in 1983, she self-published her first book, *Spoken Without a Word*. With three publishers since then, she has produced nineteen more, returning again to Turtle Hill Press® LLC, her original 'imprimatur,' for this, her 21st book on appliqué and Albums. Teaching is her pleasure, reflected in her *Beginning* and *Advanced Appliqué* DVDs (C&T Publishing). Her *Appliqué 12 Easy Ways* was translated into German, and she has produced multiple signature fabric lines with both P&B Fabrics and Robert Kaufman Textiles.

Trained in Art, History, Religion, and Education, (A.B. Wellesley College, M.S. University of Pennsylvania) Elly adores appliqué and embellishment. She designs patterns and Album quilts, stitches, teaches; researches, creates, and romances appliqué—from beloved basics to artful 'Baltimores.' Houston's Quilts, Inc. has twice displayed special Baltimore Revival exhibitions, the first—juried works inspired by Elly's books along with a retrospective of quilts by her own hand. These exhibits honored her as 2003's Silver Star Award recipient, an award given at the turn of the 20th to 21st centuries, paying respect to a specified artist for having "made a profound contribution to the contemporary Quilting Revival."

Elly has lectured at the Smithsonian Institution, the Abby Aldrich Rockefeller Museum, the American Quilt Study Group, as well as across the country and on five continents. Her seminal research paper originally published as *The Marketing of Mary Evans* (thereafter published as "Doctor Dunton, Mary Evans, and the Baltimore Album Quilt Attributions") was first presented and then published in 1989. Her work has appeared in quilt magazines in the US, Europe, and Japan, and in The Magazine Antiques, Folk Art Magazine, Victoria, Country Living, and Threads. *Elly Sienkiewicz's Beloved Baltimore Album Quilts, 25 Patterns, 12 Quilts, Appliqué Embellishments*, (2010) still in print, precedes *Spoken Without a Word 2014*.

Quilts, Inc.'s 2010 Baltimore Album Revival II exhibition accompanied their 'Baltimore's Daughters' exhibit of Elly's *Beloved Baltimore Albums*' dozen quilts, all but one designed and created under her direction. Before becoming more deeply involved with Baltimore-style group-made Albums, Elly was a 'Resident Artist' at the Glen Echo National Art Park in Glen Echo, Maryland. There she had her first (1971–76) retrospective of wall art, fabric sculptures, and earliest quilts. After the birth of her third child in 1977, Elly established Cabin Fever Calicoes, a "Quilt Shop by Mail," in business for eight years.

Quilter's Newsletter Magazine's 2009 readership voted Elly "Best Appliqué Teacher," honoring her even as her *Appliqué 12 Easy Ways!* was winning the Quilt Industry Classics Award for Best Book on Appliqué. C&T Publishing sponsored two major Baltimore Album Revival Exhibitions to celebrate Elly's books' impact on the Baltimore Album and Appliqué Revival. C&T's exhibitions produced two colorful catalogues reflecting upon the Revival at that stage—*Baltimore Album Revival* and *Baltimore Legacy*. More recently, the International Quilt Festival in Stitges, Spain, hung a display of ten of Elly's group-made Revivalist Baltimore quilts in 2012.

Elly founded The Elly Sienkiewicz Applique Academy, which celebrated its 19th year in 2014. Top-rate teaching leavened by all-Appliqué daily exhibitions, good food, and girlish fun earned 'Academy' the affectionate nickname 'Miss Tesaa.' Even friends never able to attend enjoyed following Miss Tessa on her 'List Visit' newsletter. She had begun at the Historic Inns in Annapolis, MD; moved to the Verdin Center in Lewes, DE; then spent sixteen years in Williamsburg, Virginia, at the Hospitality House and Kingsmill Resort, where her doors closed in 2014. EllySienkiewicz.net replaced its website.

Elly's Career
(but for the teaching, her greatest joy)

Cabin Fever Calicoes®, Washington, 1977–1985.

"American Country Christmas," *Quilter's Newsletter Magazine*, Nov./Dec. 1982.

✑ *Spoken Without a Word,* Turtle Hill Press, 1983.

"The American Quilt: Marking Life's Passages," *Wellesley*, Spring 1984.

"Baltimore Brides Speak Without Words," *Quilter's Newsletter Magazine*, March 1984.

"Elly Sienkiewicz: Quilting in the Baltimore Style," *Traditional Quiltworks*, Issue No. 2.

"Strip Appliqué: New Uses For an Old Technique," *American Quilter*, Fall, 1986.

"My Baltimore Album Quilt Discoveries," *Quilter's Newsletter Magazine*, May 1988.

"The World's Most Valuable Quilt: Why So Expen$ive?" *Quilting Today*, Issue No. 12.

✑ *Baltimore Beauties and Beyond: Studies in Classic Album Quilt Appliqué, Vol I,* C&T, 1989.

"The Marketing of Mary Evans," *Uncoverings 1989,* Volume 10 of the Research Papers of the American Quilt Study Group, Edited by Laurel Horton.

"Victorian Album Quilts," *Quilter's Newsletter Magazine*, Nov./Dec. 1989.

"Wreath of Hearts," *Stitch 'N Sew Quilts*, Jan./Feb. 1990.

✑ *Baltimore Album Quilts, Historic Notes & Antique Patterns,* C&T, 1990.

"Roses for Hans Christian Andersen" quilt on exhibit at *Hans Christian Andersen Museum*, Odense, Denmark; *Patchwork & Quilt Expo*, 1990. Framed appliqué donated to museum.

"The Numsen Family Quilt: Fancy Flowers From Old Baltimore," *Quilter's Newsletter Magazine*, Jan. 1990.

"Elly Sienkiewicz, Quiltmaker," *Quilts Japan*, Jan. 1990.

✑ *Baltimore Beauties and Beyond: Studies in Classic Album Quilt Appliqué, Vol. 2.* C&T, 1991.

"Penwork Plain and Fancy," *Quilter's Newsletter Magazine*, March 1991.

"Fancy Flowers, Part 1 of 3," *Quilter's Newsletter Magazine*, April 1991.

"Fancy Flowers, Part 2 of 3," *Quilter's Newsletter Magazine*, May 1991.

PHOTO: SUSAN SILVERMAN

Cabin Fever Calicoes® quiltshop by mail was begun by neighbors, Elly and Betty Martin, here with their families. Monthly space ads in *Quilters Newsletter Magazine*, sold CFC's books, notions, and solid color cottons. After Betty retired, Elly sold CFC through a Wall Street Journal classified. Her husband, mother-in-law, and children then supported and encouraged her teaching and lecturing on five continents. Retiring this year, she cherishes fond recollections of "all who peopled that paradise of teaching grown-up women (and a few men.)"

✑ Books and DVDs

"Fancy Flowers, Part 3," *Quilter's Newsletter Magazine*, June 1991.

"Picture Blocks: Capturing the Moment Then as Now," *Quilter's Newsletter Magazine*, Dec. 1991.

⚬ *Applique 12 Easy Ways!: Charming Quilts, Giftable Projects, and Timeless Techniques*, C&T, 1991.

"A Quilter's Odyssey," *Victoria Magazine*, Sept. 1992.

⚬ *Design a Baltimore Album Quilt: A Teach-Yourself Course in Sets and Borders*, C&T. 1992.

"Flowers From Baltimore Albums," *Threads Magazine*, Dec.1992/Jan.1993.

"Ribbon Roses for Elegant Appliqué," *Quilter's Newsletter Magazine*, March 1993.

"The Happiness is in the Journey," *Quilter's Newsletter Magazine*, Sept. 1993.

⚬ *Dimensional Applique: Baskets, Blooms & Baltimore Borders*, C&T 1993.

Designed *Baltimore Beauties* 46-piece fabric line, P & B Textiles, 1993.

⚬ *Applique 12 Borders and Medallions!: Patterns from Easy to Heirloom*, C&T, 1994.

"Albums, Artizans, and Odd Fellows," cover article *Folk Art Magazine*, Spring 1994.

Lecture, *Maryland Historical Society*, June 1994.

"Are Quilts Art?" *American Quilter Magazine*, Fall 1994.

⚬ *Baltimore Album Revival!: Historic Quilts in the Making, Catalogue of C&T Publishing's Baltimore Album Revival Quilt Show and Contest, Lancaster Host Hotel, Lancaster, PA* (Rita Barber's Conference), C&T, 1994.

Louise McCormick Gibney, "Baltimore Album Revival! Historic Quilts in the Making: Elly Sienkiewicz and Her Apecial Quilters," *Traditional Quilter*, January 1995.

The Elly Sienkiewicz Appliqué Academy®LLC, 1995–2014.

⚬ *Papercuts and Plenty (Baltimore Beauties and Beyond: Studies in Classic Album Quilt Appliqué, Vol. 3)*, C&T, 1995.

"Fusible Appliqué Finished With a Flourish," *Quilter's Newsletter Magazine*, June 1995.

⚬ *Romancing Ribbons into Flowers*, EZ Quilting by Wrights, 1996.

⚬ *Appliqué Paper Greetings*, American Quilter's Society, 1997.

⚬ *Baltimore Album Legacy, Catalogue of C&T Publishing's Baltimore Album Revival Quilt Show and Contest, Pacific International Quilt Show, Santa Clara, CA* (Mancuso Brothers Conference), C&T, 1998.

"Mixed Media Appliqué," *Quilter's Newsletter Magazine*, June 1998.

⚬ *Fancy Applique: 12 Lessons to Enhance Your Skills*, C&T, 1999.

"Quilts and the Stories They Tell," *American Patchwork & Quilting*, August 1999.

⚬ *The Best of Baltimore Beauties: 95 Patterns for Album Blocks and Borders*, C&T, 2000.

Jennifer Rounds, "Elly Sienkiewicz: An American Beauty," *The Quilter*, July 2001.

⚬ *The Best of Baltimore Beauties, Part II: More Patterns for Album Blocks*, C&T, 2002.

⚬ *Sweet Dreams Moon Baby: A Quilt to Make, A Story to Read*, C&T. 2003.

"Baltimore Album Review I" exhibit: Elly's one-woman invitational show of 12 quilts, honoring her as the recipient of the *Silver Star Award*, International Quilt Festival, Houston, 2003.

"Another Star Shines in Houston," *Quilter's Newsletter Magazine*, October 2003.

"What is the Fascination with Baltimore Album Quilts?" Lecture, Baltimore Museum of Art, Baltimore, MD, 2004.

"Silhouette Portraits," *Simply Quilts*, HGTV, 2004.

"Quiltmaking + Greeting Cards = Scrapbooking," *American Quilter Magazine*, Spring 2005.

"Still Speaking Without Words," *Designers' Quarters Magazine*, Summer 2005.

Designed *Spoken Without a Word* fabric line, Robert Kaufman Fabrics 2005.

"Art of Quilting Baltimore Album," *Fons & Porter's Love of Quilting*, March/April 2006.

"Come Stitch the Past to the Future," *Appliqué Quilts*, June 2006.

Mary K. Tozer, "A Conversation With Elly," *The Appliqué Society*, Nov./Dec. 2006.